2007

Enjoy This Title

The Nashua Public Library is free to all
cardholders. If you live, work, pay taxes,
or are a full-time student in Nashua you
qualify for a library card.

Increase the library's usefulness by returning
material on or before the 'date due.'

If you've enjoyed your experience with
the library and its many resources and
services, please tell others.

@ Nashua Public Library
2 Court Street, Nashua, NH 03060
603-589-4600, www.nashua.lib.nh.us

J

GAYLORD RG

CALVIN COOLIDGE

PRESIDENTIAL ✦ LEADERS

CALVIN COOLIDGE

RUTH TENZER FELDMAN

TWENTY-FIRST CENTURY BOOKS/MINNEAPOLIS

To Guinevere Poochessa, for her abiding patience

Twenty-First Century Books
A division of Lerner Publishing Group
241 First Avenue North
Minneapolis, MN 55401 U.S.A.

Website address: www.lernerbooks.com

Library of Congress Cataloging-in-Publication Data

Feldman, Ruth Tenzer.
  Calvin Coolidge / by Ruth Tenzer Feldman.
    p.   cm. — (Presidential leaders)
  Includes bibliographical references and index.
  ISBN-13: 978–0–8225–1496–1 (lib. bdg. : alk. paper)
  ISBN-10: 0–8225–1496–6 (lib. bdg. : alk. paper)
    1. Coolidge, Calvin, 1872–1933—Juvenile literature. 2. Presidents—United States—Biography—Juvenile literature. I. Title. II. Series.
  E792.F45 2007
  973.91'5'092—dc22   2005004331

Manufactured in the United States of America
1 2 3 4 5 6 – JR – 12 11 10 09 08 07

CONTENTS

———— ✦ ————

INTRODUCTION..7

1 **A VERMONT CHILDHOOD**...............................9

2 **WIDENING WORLD**...23

3 **HARD WORK AND LUCK**..............................35

4 **MR. PRESIDENT**...53

5 **FOUR MORE YEARS**......................................69

6 **RETURNING TO THE PEOPLE**......................87

TIMELINE..102

SOURCE NOTES...105

SELECTED BIBLIOGRAPHY................................107

FURTHER READING AND WEBSITES 108

INDEX...110

Plymouth Notch, Vermont, photographed in the late 1800s.
Calvin Coolidge grew up in this small town.

INTRODUCTION

Do you know, I've never really grown up?
—Calvin Coolidge, confiding in
his friend and mentor Frank W. Stearns

As the moon shone on the last hours of July 3, 1885, John Calvin Coolidge and other Plymouth Notch boys dragged a five-hundred-pound cannon from its hiding place in John Wilder's garage. Wilder had helped to steal the cannon from Plymouth Union a few days earlier. They wheeled the iron gun up the road on its old wooden carriage and got ready to welcome the Fourth of July in Vermont with a bang.

The cannon once belonged in the Notch when the annual Plymouth Township meetings were held there. But the main road was rerouted in the 1850s. After that, it became easier to hold township meetings in Union, a larger settlement a few miles away. Union folks insisted that the cannon be moved along with the meetings. Every year, boys from the Notch tried to steal the cannon back for Independence Day. This time victory was theirs.

Calvin—everyone called him Calvin or Cal—helped excitedly as the Notch raiders loaded the cannon with gunpowder and fuses. They fired thirteen blasts at about midnight, in honor of the thirteen original colonies and, coincidentally, Calvin's thirteenth birthday.

Except for his bright red hair and freckles, Calvin looked a lot like his mother, who had died that March. She had been sick for most of Calvin's life, suffering from consumption (a lung disease that we know as tuberculosis). Unlike his large, healthy father and younger sister, Calvin was small and thin for his age. He ate little, rarely played sports, and had respiratory problems and frequent colds. Consumption was the leading cause of death in the United States then. The disease seemed to run in families and often struck young adults. Folks figured Calvin would die soon too.

Calvin was a shy boy who kept to himself, even more so since his mother's death. He didn't usually hang around with the neighbors. But Calvin loved practical jokes. He carried them out whenever he could. Stealing the cannon from Plymouth Union and firing triumphantly at the Notch was the biggest, longest-running practical joke around.

Cannon raiders commented on how happy and excited Calvin looked that night. There is no record that the Notch boys had been able to steal the cannon from the Union boys during Calvin's earlier years. Perhaps this was Calvin's first time helping them. If he had his way, it wouldn't be the last.

CHAPTER ONE

A VERMONT CHILDHOOD

*It would be hard to imagine better
surroundings for the development of a boy
than those which I had. . . . Country life
does not always have breadth, but it has depth.
It is neither artificial nor superficial,
but is kept close to the realities.*

—Calvin Coolidge, on his childhood, 1929

The cannon fire that welcomed Independence Day 1885 in Plymouth Notch, Vermont, probably disturbed more cows and sheep than it did people. Three houses, a general store with a post office, a blacksmith shop, and a church made up the little town. One house belonged to Cephas Moore. Another belonged to Hiram Moor and his son-in-law John Wilder. The third was home to Moor's other son-in-law, John Coolidge. Coolidge's parents were a short walk away, and about a dozen families lived on nearby farms.

Calvin Coolidge lived in this house in Plymouth Notch until 1876.

————————————— ✧ —————————————

The man who became the thirtieth president of the United States was born into this close-knit community on July 4, 1872. He was named for his father, John Calvin Coolidge, but rarely used "John." His mother was Victoria Josephine Moor Coolidge. Coolidges and Moors (or Moores) had lived in the area for generations. Plymouth Union, up the road several miles, had about two dozen houses, several lumber mills along the Black River and, sometimes, a cannon.

Calvin's sister, Abbie (Abigail Gratia), was born on April 15, 1875, the same year Calvin fell off a horse and broke his arm. Calvin soon mended and grew to love horseback riding. His mother never seemed to recover from Abbie's birth and was sick and frail for most of Calvin's childhood. It's not clear when she came down with tuberculosis.

Young Calvin at the age of three
——————— ✧

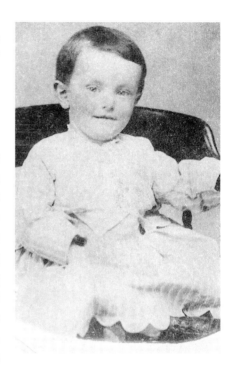

In 1876 the Coolidges moved from their home—a small, red house that was attached to the general store—to a larger home just across the street. In the following year, Calvin began attending classes at Plymouth Notch's one-room schoolhouse. Calvin started school in December, during the third term of the school year. The first term started in May and ended in early July. After a short break, students returned for the second term, which lasted from the end of August through October. The final term usually started the week after Thanksgiving and ended in late February.

Children in the Notch stayed home in the spring to help with planting and maple sugaring. Tapping the maple trees in his yard for sap was one of Calvin's favorite activities. Even his father, who was short on praise, declared Calvin an expert at getting the most sap out of a tree and producing a fine blend of maple syrup. Because his family thought Calvin was less hardy than other boys his age, they excused him from the heaviest of farm chores. When the weather was cold and rainy, they allowed him to stay indoors and read. In good weather, though, he plowed, planted, and harvested, mended stone fences, tended cattle, sheared sheep, and split firewood for the kitchen stove. Calvin worked hard and seemed to take his responsibilities seriously.

"A BIT OF AN ODD STICK"

Calvin was a quiet and hardworking student as well. The old stone schoolhouse was near the Notch, so he could walk home for lunch. About twenty to twenty-five students attended, ages five to fifteen. They sat behind two-person desks on spruce benches that lined the walls of the drafty building. In the center of the room was a smoky stove, a chalkboard, and a pail of water with a dipper. The toilets were outside the schoolhouse in unheated sheds.

At school Calvin's days were filled with memorizing facts on history, English, government, geography, arithmetic, and science. He didn't receive report cards but was known as an above-average student, steady and reliable. Only once, or so the family story goes, did Calvin act up in class. That was

✧ ─────────────
As a boy, Calvin hoped to follow in his father's footsteps as a small-town shopkeeper. He is pictured here at the age of seven.

when another boy had taken the teacher's switch (a thin, flexible branch used to whip misbehaving students) and cut it just enough so that it would break when the teacher used it. Because Calvin liked practical jokes, he misbehaved in order to get punished with the switch. When the teacher used the switch on Calvin, it broke on the first stroke.

Usually Calvin kept to himself. He got the reputation of being "a bit of an odd stick," or an unusual person. He did spend time with Thomas Moore, though, a farmer's son who lived just north of the Notch. The two hunted and fished together, ice-skated, and went sledding. Calvin joined in "bees" to husk corn, peel apples, and challenge the township's best spellers. He learned horseback riding tricks, loved animals, and wasn't afraid of physical danger. Painfully shy, his biggest source of worry seemed to be people, especially strangers.

Calvin's father had several jobs when Calvin was a child. He often was away from home. In addition to running the farm and owning Plymouth Notch's general store, John Coolidge worked as a deputy sheriff, justice of the peace (a person who performs marriages and helps judges with other legal matters), tax collector, superintendent of schools, and four-term member of the Vermont legislature (a branch of government that makes laws). John Coolidge ran a strict household, and he taught Calvin the importance of saving money. Unlike many fathers at that time, he did not physically punish his children.

Calvin's world changed dramatically when he was not quite thirteen. On March 14, 1885, his mother died. Calvin was brokenhearted. Although he continued to do his chores week after week, neighbors noticed him making daily trips to his mother's grave.

Calvin's grandmother, Sarah Almeda Coolidge, helped to raise him and Abbie. When he caught a cold, she brought him oranges—an uncommon remedy in those days and a luxury in the Coolidge household. He and Abbie spent a lot of time at her house, which was just down the road. Mattie McWain, a distant cousin, was hired to help with the household chores and make breakfast—usually coffee, rolls, and doughnuts, sometimes bacon, always pickles. A man named Warren Spaulding worked on the farm whenever Calvin's father was away, and Calvin seemed to enjoy Spaulding's company.

John Coolidge rarely missed taking his family to an annual circus extravaganza in Rutland, a bustling town of twelve thousand Vermonters a two-hour buggy ride away. In 1885 the circus came to Rutland on July 22, shortly after Calvin's cannon episode. It was a two-ring show featuring Jumbo the elephant.

That November Calvin passed a test that qualified him to be a teacher in Vermont, even though he was only thirteen years old. His father was superintendent of schools and could have hired Calvin to teach at the Notch. But John Coolidge decided that Calvin should continue his education. Calvin stayed at his school for the next term and prepared to go to Black River Academy, a school in Ludlow, Vermont, that John Coolidge had attended.

Neighbors gathered at the Coolidge house for a going-away party for Calvin, who made molasses candy for them. He packed two small bags of his best store-bought clothes and left his farm clothes at home. As Calvin and his father set out for Ludlow in their horse-drawn sleigh, the sun's light made the snow glisten. Calvin was eager to go. He later wrote, "I was perfectly certain that I was traveling out of the darkness into the light." A calf came with them, destined for Ludlow's railroad yard and a trip to Boston. John Coolidge told Calvin that if Calvin ever got to Boston, he should remember that the calf got there first.

ACADEMY DAYS

Because Ludlow was twelve miles from home, Calvin stayed there during the school term. He shared a room with Alva Peck at a boardinghouse on Main Street and was the only academy student there. Peck, twenty-seven, was a law clerk in a local firm and the son of a lawyer that John Coolidge knew.

When spring term started on February 22, 1886, Calvin met his classmates. There were about 125 students at the academy, many of whom came from Ludlow. The academy was free to Ludlow residents, but others paid. Calvin signed up for the basic course (a group of classes in English, mathematics, and other subjects). It cost fifty cents a week.

That first term, Calvin's overall grades were the lowest they ever had been or would be—83.8 points out of a possible 100. He hated algebra, his worst subject. His studies at the Notch likely hadn't prepared him well. He also had difficulty living in a large town.

On weekends Calvin often went home or visited Sarah Pollard (his mother's older sister) and her family four miles away in Proctorsville. Aunt Sarah served a big Sunday dinner and looked after him in a motherly sort of way.

After final exams in May, Calvin returned home for the summer. He had missed out on maple sugaring, a favorite activity, and he busied himself with other work on the farm. When he returned to the academy in the fall, Calvin signed up for the Latin scientific curriculum—a group of

Calvin shows off his stylish look, complete with derby hat and cane.

✧ ————————————

more difficult classes, including Latin. These classes cost sixty cents a week. Calvin began to dress in stylish, fancy clothes. He had a derby hat, polished cane, and a carefully starched shirt. Calvin's flaming red hair had turned to a lighter, sandy color, and he let it grow longer. His freckles disappeared. The most striking feature on his thin face became his blue eyes. Academy classmates called him a "dude," a word then used for a man who was overly concerned with how he looked.

Calvin still spent a lot of time by himself, although he roomed with students closer to his age and visited Peck and other law clerks in Ludlow. On Saturdays he had a job making doll carriages at the Ludlow Toy Manufacturing Company. Although he studied a lot, he did like to joke around from time to time. One Friday, when he was showing classmates a circus trick, he slipped and broke his arm. After the doctor set it, Calvin went home for the weekend and insisted on coming back on Monday so as not to miss any classes.

In 1887 Calvin signed up for the classical course, which would help him prepare to go to college. No one in Calvin's family had attended college, but John Coolidge wanted his son to go. Calvin wanted Abbie to join him at the academy, and she did in February 1888.

By the time Abbie came, Calvin had found a subject he enjoyed a great deal—the orations, or speeches, of Cicero, a famous statesman of ancient Rome. He memorized these Latin orations and recited them in class. By studying Cicero's phrases, he began to develop the skills needed to write and deliver an effective speech.

The more time Calvin spent at Black River Academy, the more comfortable and popular he became. His class-mates appreciated his practical jokes and dry humor. They elected him president of the senior class. In November 1889, a mule was locked up overnight in the classroom of an unpopular English teacher. It destroyed the furniture and left a mess all over the floor. Calvin did not admit to being involved, but he probably was.

Calvin and Abbie went home in February 1890 at the end of the winter term. About a week later, Abbie came down with a high fever and abdominal pains. Calvin returned to

Abbie (right) and her brother, Calvin, were very close friends.

the academy on March 2 for the start of the spring term but came back to the Notch with a Ludlow doctor his father had sent for on March 5. Abbie died the next day, probably of appendicitis (an inflamed appendix). About his sister, Calvin later wrote, "The memory of the charm of her presence and her dignified devotion to the right will always [be with] me."

Calvin returned to the academy to finish out his senior year. In May he graduated with four other boys and four girls. At the graduation, Calvin recited a ten-minute speech he wrote. It was called "Oratory in History." The next day, Calvin was back home, working on the farm.

——————————— ✧ ———————————

The first page of Calvin's speech "Oratory in History" is pictured below.

AN *OUDEN* AT AMHERST

The Notch had grown during Calvin's time at the academy. There was a cheese factory nearby, and John Coolidge had added a social hall above the general store. The Union boys had recaptured the cannon, and it was a relatively quiet Fourth of July. Calvin focused on his chores. He made plans to attend the University of Vermont at the end of the summer.

Three weeks before college was to start, the principal of Black River Academy told John Coolidge that a space might be open for Calvin at Amherst, a more prestigious—and more expensive—college in Massachusetts. Calvin had to pass tests in classics, history, and mathematics in order to go to school there. Calvin felt afraid when his father agreed. He wasn't sure he would pass the tests, particularly in algebra.

But John Coolidge was determined. On September 15, Calvin took the train to Amherst and nervously waited to take his exams. He came down with a bad cold and returned home without completing them. Calvin's uncle Frank had recently died of consumption, and folks in the Notch doubted that the frail teenager would survive the winter.

By March 1891, Calvin was still weak but clearly recovering. The principal suggested that he register as a senior at St. Johnsbury Academy, about fifty miles away. If he got a graduation certificate from there, Calvin could get into Amherst without taking the dreaded tests. Calvin started at St. Johnsbury on April 15, and by June he had earned his certificate.

Back on the farm for the summer, Calvin went with his father to see President Benjamin Harrison at the dedication of a monument in Bennington, Vermont. Harrison was a

Republican, as were most of the people that Calvin knew then. When he was a teen, Calvin paid close attention to his father's political activities. He later explained that "[because] of what I saw and heard in my early life, I came to have a good working knowledge of the practical side of government."

During that summer, John Coolidge fell in love with a young teacher named Caroline Athelia (Carrie) Brown—a woman thought to be "one of the finest . . . of [the] neighborhood." Shortly after his father married Carrie in September, Calvin took the train to Amherst.

Calvin rented a boardinghouse room on Pleasant Street. He shared the room with Alfred Turner, a junior, and there were no other students at the house. Alfred was an athlete, and Calvin likely went to sporting events because of his roommate. Calvin also dutifully attended gymnastics lessons four times a week. At five feet nine, Calvin still weighed only 120 pounds.

Like the rest of the forty-five freshmen in his class, Calvin had to put up with teasing from the older students. He was still quiet and shy. He made few friends and went for long walks in the woods. Calvin attended freshmen class meetings but was not invited to join any fraternities, or college social clubs. His classmates called him an *ouden* (Greek for "nothing") because he wasn't a fraternity man.

Calvin studied hard and worried he might fail. He missed the farm a great deal. Returning to Amherst after Christmas, he wrote to his father, "Each time I get home I hate to go away worse than before. . . ."

In January 1892, Calvin learned with relief that he had passed his first term exams, even algebra. By the middle of spring, his grades improved.

As a member of Amherst's Class of 1895, Calvin was invited to give a speech during Fourth of July festivities at Plymouth Notch. He was twenty years old that day, nearly an adult. After his speech, Calvin joined his neighbors as they fired off the newly recaptured cannon. Seven years earlier, he likely had little to do with stealing the cannon from Plymouth Union. This time, he was one of the leaders.

Calvin and several others had learned that the cannon was hidden in a grove behind a Union hotel. The Union boys had tied a string to the cannon and attached it to a cowbell in the hotel as an alarm. Late one night while Union folks attended a dance, raiders from the Notch carefully cut the string, dragged the cannon up the hill, and hid it in John Wilder's barn.

When Independence Day festivities ended, Calvin told the Notch boys to return the cannon's wheeled base to the barn and carry the five-hundred-pound gun into Wilder's house. They hid the cannon under Grandmother Moor's bed. There is no record that the cannon ever left the Notch again.

When Coolidge arrived in Northampton in 1895 to study law with Hammond and Field, he had no expectation of ever becoming president of the United States.

CHAPTER TWO

WIDENING WORLD

*Remaining in one office long did not appeal to
me, for I was not seeking a public career. My
heart was in the law.*
—Calvin Coolidge, 1929

Twenty-year-old Calvin Coolidge started to make friends
during his sophomore year at Amherst. He roomed with
young men about his age in a house closer to the college
and played practical jokes on the freshmen.

By his junior year, Coolidge was a highly skilled speaker. He was good in debates and had a great sense of timing.
He gave a funny speech at the Class of 1895's Plug Hat
Dinner on November 23, 1893, and soon made more
friends. They called him Cooley and asked him to join
them on trips to Boston.

Coolidge's classmates finally invited him to join a fraternity in his senior year. They also chose him to be the
Grove Orator, the student who gives a humorous speech

about what his class has accomplished at Amherst. Coolidge dressed in fine clothes, as all men in fraternities did. He bought a tuxedo for special occasions and a uniform to wear in fencing, a sport where players duel with swords. He also attended parties and tried his best at dancing.

During his last two years at Amherst, Coolidge did better in school as well. The teacher he liked the most was named Charles E. Garman. Coolidge enrolled in Garman's class as a junior and senior. The class combined psychology (the study of emotions, behavior, and the mind) and philosophy (the study of logic, reason, and ideas). Garman discussed Charles Darwin's theory of evolution—a very controversial subject then—and asked his students to read and analyze many books. Like many fellow classmates, Coolidge came away from Garman's class with a deep religious faith and a strong belief in serving others. "We looked on Garman as a man who walked with God," he later wrote.

On June 26, 1895, Coolidge and his seventy-five or so classmates gathered outside. Coolidge delivered his Grove Oration to great success. The next day, with his father in the audience, Coolidge graduated from Amherst cum laude (with honors).

LEARNING THE LAW

After graduation Coolidge decided to study law. He became a clerk in the law firm of John C. Hammond and Henry P. Field, both Amherst graduates. The firm was in Northampton, Massachusetts, a town of twenty-three thousand people a few miles from Amherst and home to Smith

College. Coolidge wrote to his father that Northampton was small enough so that the cost of living would not be too high but large enough to offer career possibilities.

Both lawyers encouraged Coolidge in his studies. He worked on legal documents during the day. At night he read speeches by Daniel Webster, one of the United States' greatest orators, and he translated some of Cicero's orations from their original Latin. He also enjoyed reading Shakespeare's plays, as well as poems, novels, and essays.

Coolidge entered his own essay in a national contest sponsored by the Sons of the American Revolution (an organization for the descendants of men who participated in the American Revolution, 1775–1783). He had written the essay—which was called "The Principles Fought for in the American Revolution"—during his senior year at Amherst. Coolidge won first place and received a gold medal worth $150. Hammond read about the prize in the newspaper and asked Coolidge why he hadn't mentioned it. Coolidge responded that he didn't think Hammond would be interested. Coolidge was still a private person who preferred to keep to himself.

Hammond and Field were outgoing and well-connected employers. They introduced Coolidge to the political life of Northampton. Coolidge handed out ballots for Field, whom the Republican Party had chosen to run for mayor of Northampton. He also met with other Republicans to decide on a candidate for state senator, and he wrote political articles in local newspapers. On June 29, 1897, Field brought Coolidge before a panel of three judges. The judges questioned Coolidge to see how much he knew about Massachusetts law. Field asked the judges to allow his young clerk to become a lawyer, and on July 2 they did. Coolidge later wrote, "Only after I [became a lawyer] did I notify my father. He had expected that my studies would take another year, and I wanted to surprise him if I succeeded and not disappoint him if I failed. I did not fail. I was just twenty-five years old and very happy."

Coolidge spent eight hundred dollars to buy furniture and law books, and he opened his own law office on Main Street in February 1898. He originally became involved in politics as a way to find clients and help his career. And, remembering Garman's teaching at Amherst, he wanted to serve the public. On December 6, he was elected to be city councilman from Northampton's Ward 2 (a particular section of the city). The position did not pay, but it gave Coolidge the chance to meet some of the town's most important people.

Coolidge continued to work hard and deal honestly—when he wasn't playing practical jokes. He continued to improve his writing and speaking skills. He discovered that speech could be a powerful political tool.

In 1900 Coolidge was elected to be city solicitor (a lawyer who argues cases on behalf of the city). He was elected again in 1901. Coolidge lost the 1902 race for city solicitor, one of the rare times he would lose an election.

In June 1903, Coolidge was appointed to work for six months as the clerk of courts (assistant to judges) for Hampshire County. He decided not to stay in the position. Instead, he continued in his law practice. "Had I decided otherwise," he later wrote, "I could have had much more peace of mind in the last twenty-five years."

In 1904 Coolidge became chairman of Northampton's Republican City Committee. He lived in Robert Weir's boardinghouse near a school for the hearing impaired, called Clarke School for the Deaf. Shaving near a window one morning, he heard a young woman's laughter. At the time, he was wearing his long underwear and a hat. He discovered that the source of the laughter was Grace Anna Goodhue, who was a teacher at Clarke. Overcoming his usual shyness, Coolidge arranged to be introduced to her.

FAMILY AND CAREER

Grace was high-spirited and lively, an outgoing woman with thick black hair, a quick smile, and lots of charm. She had attended the University of Vermont and had a college degree (which was very unusual for a woman of her time). She also was a member of Phi Beta

─────────── ✧

Grace Goodhue was teaching lip-reading to children in Northampton when Coolidge met her in 1904.

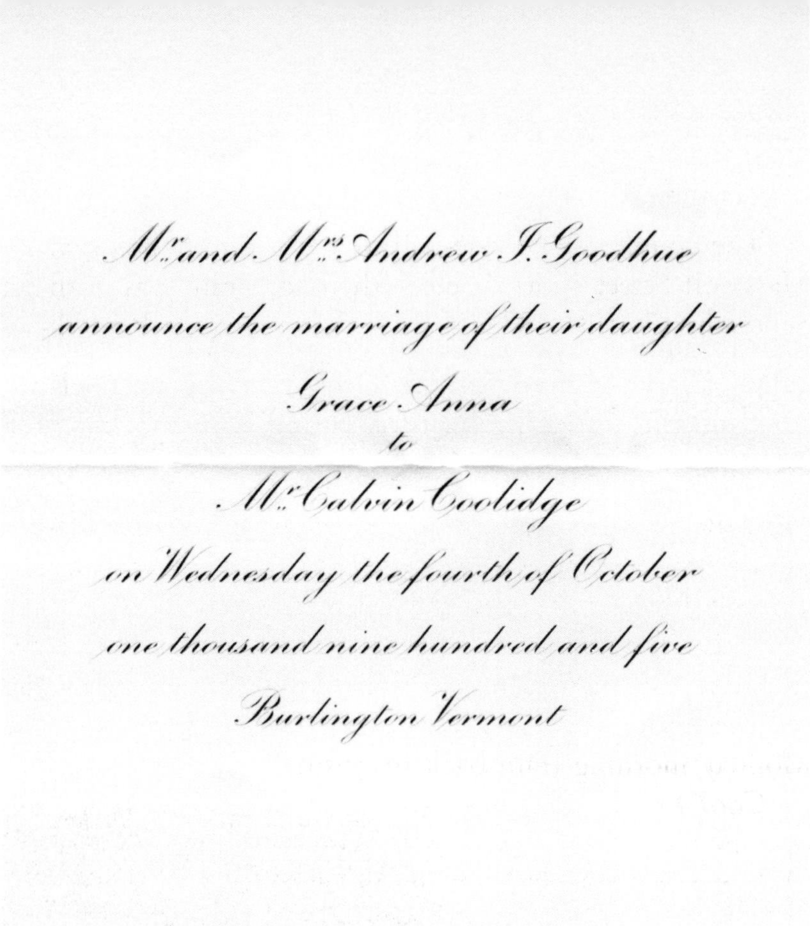

Mr. and Mrs. Andrew I. Goodhue

announce the marriage of their daughter

Grace Anna

to

Mr. Calvin Coolidge

on Wednesday the fourth of October

one thousand nine hundred and five

Burlington Vermont

The invitation to Coolidge and Grace Goodhue's 1905 wedding

———————————— ✧ ————————————

Kappa, a national society for students of high academic standing. Grace wrote to a friend about Calvin, "He is quiet and doesn't say much but what he does say amounts to something." Coolidge later wrote, "We thought we were made for each other."

On October 4, 1905, they were married in Grace's home in Burlington, Vermont. He was thirty-three years old, and she was twenty-six. They spent a short honeymoon in Montreal, Canada, before returning to Northampton. Coolidge ran for the school board but was defeated in December. He thought the reason might be that he had no children.

The couple rented one-half of a two-family house at 21 Massasoit Street shortly before their son John was born on September 7, 1906. That fall Coolidge ran as a Republican for a seat in the Massachusetts House of Representatives. He won by just 264 votes and never lost another election.

To be closer to his job at the statehouse in Boston, Coolidge left his family in Northampton and rented a small room at the Adams House, an inexpensive hotel in Boston. He bought an extra suit and started on his career as a reliable, hardworking follower of Republican leaders. He learned a lot from W. Murray Crane, who was a U.S. senator from Massachusetts at that time. On weekends he returned to Grace and their new baby, then took the Monday morning train back to Boston.

Coolidge served a second one-year term as a state representative but decided against a third term. During his two years, he tried to improve the lives of low-income workers. He supported pensions, or government

———————— ✧

Baby John Coolidge, seated on the lap of his nursemaid (and the Coolidge's housekeeper), Sophia Richardson

payments for retired teachers and the widows and families of firefighters. He also supported a six-day workweek (rather than seven!), shorter work hours for women and children, and cheaper streetcar fares for schoolchildren. Coolidge helped to pass a bill requiring the installation of medical equipment in factories. The factories were unsafe, and workers were often hurt on the job.

On the national level, Coolidge supported voting rights for women and the direct election of U.S. senators by the citizens within each state. At that time, state legislatures usually chose these men. (There wouldn't be a woman senator until 1922, and she held the job for just twenty-four hours—in between the death of Senator Tom Watson and the election of his replacement, Senator Walter George.) Several years later, both of these proposals were realized. The Constitution's seventeenth Amendment provided for direct elections of senators, and the nineteenth Amendment gave citizens the right to vote regardless of their sex.

Coolidge's second child, Calvin Jr., was born in Northampton on April 13, 1908, while Coolidge was finishing his second term in the state legislature. Next was Coolidge's 1909 campaign for mayor of Northampton. Coolidge contacted many voters personally and bought them drinks and cigars. He won by 165 votes.

MAYOR AND MORE
The election to mayor was an important turning point in Coolidge's life. "On the first Monday of January, 1910," Coolidge later wrote, "I began a public career that was to continue until the first Monday of March, 1929, when it was to end by my own [choice]."

Coolidge served two terms as mayor, from January 1910 through the end of 1911. He lowered Northampton's taxes, improved its streets and sidewalks, expanded its police force, and cut its debt. Coolidge also raised pay for teachers. When a state senator decided to retire, Coolidge ran for his seat. Well-known local Republicans supported him, and he managed to win another close race. He returned to the Adams House in Boston and once again set about serving the Commonwealth of Massachusetts. Coolidge's skill and reputation for quietly getting things done continued to grow.

During his first term as state senator, Coolidge chaired the Special Conciliation Committee, which helped to settle a strike—or protest in which workers refuse to work—of thirty thousand textile mill workers. Reelected in 1912, Coolidge chaired a committee on railroads and worked to pass a bill allowing the New Haven, Connecticut, trolley line to expand to Northampton and other places in western Massachusetts.

Senator Crane, who had known Coolidge since Coolidge's first days in the Massachusetts House of Representatives, became interested. He is said to have commented to a businessperson going to visit Northampton, "Find out all you can about a young man named Coolidge there. You will save trouble in looking him up! He is one of the coming men of this country."

Coolidge decided to run for a third term in the Massachusetts Senate. After he won, he discovered an important political opportunity. The president of the senate did not win reelection, mostly because he didn't believe that women should have the right to vote. With Crane's help,

Coolidge became president of the senate. This made him the state's highest-ranking Republican officeholder.

"HAVE FAITH IN MASSACHUSETTS"

In January of 1914, Coolidge gave an acceptance speech to members of the senate. According to Coolidge, "a spirit of radicalism [had taken over] which unless [controlled] was likely to [become] very destructive." He wanted to "appeal to the conservative spirit of the people" with the message that hard work and faith in democracy would create a better life for all Americans. The speech was soon called "Have Faith in Massachusetts." It showed Coolidge's philosophy and his simple but strong speaking style. Here's a portion:

> We need a broader, firmer, deeper faith in the people—a faith that men desire to do right. . . . Man has a spiritual nature. Touch it, and it must respond as the magnet responds to the pole. To that, not to selfishness, let the laws of the Commonwealth appeal. . . . Let the laws of Massachusetts proclaim to her humblest citizen, performing the most [common] task, . . . the recognition that all men are peers, . . . the recognition that all work is glorified. Such is the path to equality before the law.

Quiet and careful, Coolidge knew how to work with other members of the legislature. Coolidge made sure that the business of the senate was done efficiently. He was reelected to the office in 1915 and gave a forty-two-word

Coolidge poses with his wife, Grace, and his two sons, Calvin Jr. (middle left) *and John* (middle right).

✧

speech to his fellow senators about the importance of being brief.

Another opportunity opened up in the fall of 1915. Massachusetts governor David Walsh was a Democrat, and his second-in-command, Lieutenant Governor Grafton Cushing, was a Republican. Cushing wanted to run for the governorship in 1915 and so did another important Republican named Samuel McCall. Neither man was willing to run for lieutenant governor. That left the spot open for Calvin Coolidge.

Coolidge wasn't sure he wanted to run. But Republican leaders such as Crane said that he would be on a winning ticket. Frank Waterhouse Stearns, who owned a Boston dry goods store and who had also graduated from Amherst, offered to manage much of the campaign. Coolidge's plain ways balanced the polished, professional style of Samuel McCall, a businessperson, former newspaper editor, and U.S. congressman. Coolidge agreed.

People who knew about Coolidge's lack of charm joked that McCall could fill any hall in Massachusetts and Coolidge could empty it. But Crane declared, "That Yankee twang . . . will be worth a hundred thousand votes." Crane turned out to be at least half right. Coolidge beat his Democratic opponent by about fifty-two thousand votes.

CHAPTER THREE

HARD WORK AND LUCK

*[W]hen a duty comes to us, with it a power
comes to enable us to perform it.*
—Calvin Coolidge, 1929

January 9, 1916, marked the start of three one-year terms
Calvin Coolidge served as lieutenant governor of
Massachusetts. Unlike lieutenant governors of other states,
Coolidge was not in charge of the Massachusetts Senate.
He led Governor McCall's advisory council, which dealt
with matters involving finances, state jobs, orphanages, pris-
ons, and other state institutions. He gave speeches to gain
support for World War I (1914–1918) when the United
States entered the conflict in April 1917.

The Coolidges continued to live in their rented house
in Northampton. Since Grace Coolidge was very busy as
the wife of the lieutenant governor, a housekeeper joined
the family. Ralph W. Hemenway took over part of
Coolidge's law practice as his partner.

As governor of Massachusetts, Coolidge decreased the workweek hours of women and children, supported higher pay standards for public employees, and set up a state budget.

✧ ——————————

Frank Stearns, the Boston businessperson who had supported Coolidge when he was running for lieutenant governor, continued to help him. Stearns hadn't liked Coolidge when they first met in 1913, but he grew to admire Coolidge's reliability, efficiency, and quiet manner. Stearns, who was about twenty years older than Coolidge, was eager to see the younger man make it to the top in politics, maybe even become president. He introduced the lieutenant governor to important people, gave his family gifts, entertained them, and covered Coolidge's political expenses. Stearns once offered Coolidge five thousand dollars, but Coolidge gave the money back.

"It was no secret I desired to be Governor," Coolidge later wrote. When Samuel McCall decided to retire from the governorship after three terms, he encouraged Coolidge to take his place. Coolidge easily won his party's nomination for governor.

Statewide campaigning was more difficult for Coolidge. "It's a hard thing for me to play this game," he told Stearns.

"In politics one must meet people. . . . I'm all right with old friends, but every time I meet a stranger . . . it's not easy."

The influenza (flu) outbreak of 1918 forced Massachusetts Republicans to cancel their state convention (a political meeting to select candidates for office). The Republican Party was split between those who, like Coolidge, supported President Wilson's decision to send troops to fight in World War I and those who attacked the president's actions. But the Democratic nominee, Richard H. Long, had little political experience or support. Coolidge managed to beat Long by 16,773 votes.

THE GOVERNOR AND THE STRIKE

Calvin Coolidge officially became governor of the Commonwealth of Massachusetts on New Year's Day 1919. The celebration included cannons booming a twenty-one-gun salute. Coolidge had come a long way from his Fourth of July cannon pranks at Plymouth Notch.

Massachusetts did not provide a place for its governors to live. The Coolidges decided to stay in Northampton rather than rent a house in Boston. The new governor took a simple two-room suite with bath on the third floor of the Adams House. The suite cost about $3.50 a day. Grace Coolidge sometimes joined her husband there but usually stayed in Northampton. She is said to have remarked, "Mr. Coolidge may be governor of Massachusetts but I shall be first of all the mother of my sons."

Coolidge saved most of the ten thousand dollars he earned each year as governor. He continued to have two suits (one for business, one for travel) and a set of formal clothes. At a time when automobiles were very popular, he still didn't buy a car.

COOLIDGE AND CARS

"It's wonderful to ride in a horseless wagon," Calvin Coolidge is said to have remarked after he took his first automobile ride, "But it won't amount to much!"

That was in 1904, when Coolidge was clerk of the court in Massachusetts. He bumped along winding roads in the Berkshire Mountains with his neighbor Fred Jager at the wheel of the only gasoline-powered car in Northampton. The car might have been a one-cylinder, three-horsepower Oldsmobile or one of automaker Henry Ford's early models that rolled off the assembly line when the Ford Motor Company started in 1903.

Assembly lines were key to the development of the automobile industry. Each worker on the line was responsible

A row of cars at the Ford plant await sale and delivery.

Henry Ford
──────────────── ✧

for one manufacturing task. This technique reduced the time it took to build a car and brought the price of a car down to a level many Americans could afford. Ford invented his practical and inexpensive Model T in 1908, and the automobile industry started booming.

By 1924 Henry Ford's cars were so popular that there was a Ford-for-President movement. Coolidge won the election but lost his prediction about the automobile. There were an estimated 19 million cars in the United States in 1924, when the nation had about 114 million people. The "horseless wagon" had definitely amounted to a lot!

With Republican Channing Cox as lieutenant governor, Coolidge set about the business of governing Massachusetts. As quiet as ever, he rarely showed emotions in public. He often seemed tired and tense. Despite taking a variety of medicines, he continued to have the breathing problems he had as a child.

While in Boston, Coolidge took a walk every day with his bodyguard, Edward Horrigan, and worked closely with his secretary, Henry Long. He spoke very little to either man. Coolidge's office in the statehouse was large and elegant. His glass-topped mahogany desk was always neat and had on it a picture of his mother.

Barely one week after Coolidge took office, Frank Stearns wrote to Dwight Morrow, who had been one year behind Coolidge at Amherst. By 1919 Morrow was a rich partner in the Wall Street firm of J. P. Morgan and Company. Stearns suggested that the two of them form a sort of Coolidge-for-President committee, and Morrow agreed. Coolidge's political career was quickly gaining momentum.

In the summer of 1919, an incident with the Boston police force added to the governor's growing reputation. Boston's police officers worked long hours under poor conditions for low pay. Many on the force wanted to form a police officers' union (a group that would work for the rights of the officers). But their boss, Commissioner Edwin Curtis, ordered them not to do so. On August 11, 1919, the police disobeyed their boss's order. Commissioner Curtis refused to recognize the union and charged the nineteen union leaders with insubordination, or refusal to obey. They were found guilty at a hearing, but their sentences were postponed. The police threatened to strike.

Police commissioner Curtis stands behind his desk during the Boston police strikes of 1919.
─────────────── ✧

Commissioner Curtis said he would not back down.

Boston's mayor, Andrew J. Peters, sided with the commissioner. He assured Governor Coolidge that the matter could be settled without him. Coolidge said he sympathized with the police but disapproved of a strike. He also said he would not interfere in the dispute.

On September 7, Commissioner Curtis suspended the nineteen union leaders from the police force without pay. On September 8, the Boston police voted 1,134 to 2 to strike the next day. Front-page headlines on the September 9 *Boston Globe* announced that a strike was set for 5:45 P.M. Still, neither side would compromise. That evening 1,117 of the city's 1,544 police officers refused to go on duty.

Lawlessness took to the streets of Boston. Some of the crimes—such as openly gambling with dice—were relatively minor. Others—such as robbery and looting— were serious. Mayor Peters sent in citizens with military training to restore order and asked Coolidge to send in even more men.

On September 10, local troops patrolled the city. By the time Coolidge sent in reinforcements the next day, the worst was over. Curtis and Peters fired the strikers.

President Wilson congratulated Coolidge on the way he handled the strike. The next day, Coolidge announced that the strikers should not be rehired. The strikers never got their jobs back.

Replying on September 14 to a telegram from Samuel Gompers (president of a national workers' group called the

———————————— ◇ ————————————

The National Guard patrols Boston during the 1919 police strike. Coolidge's handling of the strike earned him public support and admiration.

American Federation of Labor), Coolidge wrote, "There is no right to strike against the public safety by anybody, anywhere, any time." Coolidge's response to the strike made him very popular. Some Americans believed that strikes were dangerous. Since strikes could cause disorder, some saw them as a threat to the smooth operation of government. A political revolution in Russia had brought a Communist government to power there in 1917. Communism was very different from the U.S. democratic system of government, and many found it threatening. Anyone who seemed to be questioning U.S. government was in danger of being labeled a Communist. When Coolidge spoke out against the strikers, he became the symbol of a law-and-order official. Many Americans believed that he and officials like him could protect the country from Communism.

The Coolidge-for-President committee jumped into action. Stearns published a collection of Coolidge's speeches featuring "Have Faith in Massachusetts." Coolidge later wrote that the effect of that speech "was beyond my expectation."

On November 4, Coolidge won reelection by a large majority (317,774 to 192,673) over Democratic candidate Richard Long. Many thought the Boston police strike was the reason why.

Prohibition took effect in the United States on January 16, 1920, shortly after Coolidge started his second term as governor. Prohibition made it illegal to manufacture, sell, or transport liquor in the United States. Coolidge followed the law strictly. He did not tolerate any beer, wine, or liquor publicly or privately.

Coolidge also strictly followed an order from the Massachusetts legislature to reduce the size of government.

He cut the number of state agencies and bureaus from 118 to 20. "I am glad it is done," he later told his secretary. "It is the worst job I ever had to do!"

Coolidge's stepmother died in May 1920. Afterward, Coolidge seemed less interested in running for president. He stayed in Boston when the Republican National Convention opened in Chicago, Illinois, three weeks later. Stearns sent a copy of Coolidge's speeches to every delegate (person selected to cast votes) at the convention. The

————————————— ✧ —————————————

Despite staying home from the 1920 Republican National Convention, Coolidge was nominated for the vice presidency.

speeches were later collected in a book called *Have Faith in Massachusetts*.

Coolidge was nominated for the presidency, but he received only a few votes. None of the three major candidates (Leonard Wood, Frank Lowden, and Hiram Johnson) had enough votes to win. Party members at the convention finally agreed to choose Ohio senator Warren G. Harding. The next national election was the first in which women could vote, and the Republican politicians thought that Harding's charm and good looks would get him votes.

Coolidge had neither charm nor good looks, but he was a strong law-and-order candidate. Delegate Wallace McCamant of Oregon put Coolidge's name in the ring for vice president, and convention members quickly chose Coolidge (674 votes to 146 votes) over Irvine L. Lenroot. After the long balloting for president during a hot and costly stay in Chicago, everyone was ready to pick a vice president and go home.

Coolidge was disappointed at not winning the nomination for president, but he decided to campaign as Harding's running mate. Their opposition, Democrats James M. Cox for president and Franklin Delano Roosevelt for vice president, didn't stand a chance. Americans seemed ready for a Republican president. President Wilson, a Democrat, had failed to carry out an effective peace program after World War I. On November 2, Harding and Coolidge won easily, by a margin of almost two to one.

Coolidge ended his term as governor of Massachusetts on January 6, 1921. Channing Cox, who had been his lieutenant governor, took his place. Coolidge shook hands and

*In Washington, D.C., Coolidge (right) shakes hands with Harding,
his running mate, for the first time ever.*

said good-bye to many supporters in Northampton, and the
family headed for Washington, D.C., to find a place to live.
The Coolidges stayed at a hotel called the Willard, renting
a suite of four rooms recently occupied by former vice president Thomas Marshall and his wife. The Coolidge children—John, fourteen, and Calvin Jr., twelve—began classes
at a school called Mercersburg Academy, in Pennsylvania.

On March 4, Coolidge took the vice-presidential oath
of office and attended President Harding's inauguration (the
ceremony at which Harding was sworn in as president).
Since Coolidge held such a high office, people expected
him and his wife to go to lots of dinners. Coolidge liked
the fact that as vice president, he could arrive late and leave

early. Still a shy man who spoke very little, Coolidge became known as Silent Cal. The story goes that at one dinner a woman said to him, "You must talk to me, Mr. Coolidge. I made a bet today that I could get more than two words out of you." Coolidge answered, "You lose."

The cost of living in Washington was a strain for a man used to living on a small amount of money. Coolidge later wrote, "[M]y experience has convinced me that an official residence . . . should be provided for the Vice-President."

As part of his political duties, Coolidge was in charge of the Senate. He described this job as "fascinating." And he noted, "I soon found that the Senate had [only] one . . . rule . . . which was . . . that the Senate would do anything it wanted to do whenever it wanted to do it. When I learned that, I did not waste much time on the other rules, because they were so seldom applied."

COOLIDGE LUCK

Coolidge also gave speeches, much as he did when he helped to govern Massachusetts. He kept up his ties to Massachusetts. In May he was elected to serve on the board of trustees (managers) of Amherst College for the rest of his life. People who watched his rise in state politics joked about Coolidge luck. Officeholders had left jobs that Coolidge filled in election after election. Some wondered out loud whether Harding would finish his term as president.

Harding included Coolidge in meetings with his cabinet (top advisers). The vice president said little but listened carefully. He learned what the American public would soon find out—that many dishonest people were working for Harding.

Coolidge (second from right, seated) *was an important member of President Harding's cabinet. Harding is seated third from the right.*

———————————— ◇ ————————————

On May 31, 1921, Harding signed Executive Order 3474. The order involved three plots of oil-rich land. The government owned the land and was reserving it for the U.S. Navy to use to fuel its ships in case of an emergency. Two of the plots were in California. The third was in Salt Creek, Wyoming. The land in Wyoming was known as Teapot Dome because it looked a little like the top of a teapot. Congress had put the land under the control of the secretary of the navy in 1920.

Businesspeople wanted the land so that they could remove and sell the oil that lay under it. They pressured those who worked for Harding, including Secretary of the Interior Albert Fall, to give control of the land to them.

Fall convinced President Harding that the Department of the Interior should be in charge of all oil reserves. Executive Order 3474 shifted control of the land from the secretary of the navy to the secretary of the interior.

Secretary Fall was now in charge of the land. He arranged for Edward Doheny, a businessperson who owned Pan-American Petroleum and Transport Company, to lease—or pay to use—some of the property in California. Several months later, in April 1922, Fall secretly leased the land known as the Teapot Dome to Harry Sinclair, another oil company owner. Oil that should have been saved for

——————————— ✧ ———————————

The Teapot Dome oil field in Wyoming was the cause of a large scandal during the Harding administration.

military emergencies would be sold to consumers to make businesspeople wealthy.

Other dishonest activities also came to light. In November, shortly after President Harding voted against giving more money to veterans, the public learned that government workers were illegally making money on sales of goods belonging to the Veterans Bureau. From his post as president of the Senate, Coolidge watched as senators demanded an investigation of these activities.

Early in 1923, Albert Fall resigned from his job. The Veterans Bureau's lawyer, Charles Cramer, and bureau director Charles Forbes also resigned. In March, Cramer committed

———————————— ✧ ————————————

In 1922 President Harding vetoes (refuses to approve) the veterans bill.

suicide. Jess Smith, who was Attorney General Daugherty's personal secretary, committed suicide in May. Rumor had it that Smith was involved in dishonest activities.

Congress adjourned, and many people in Washington got ready to leave for the summer. President Harding seemed to be under stress from recent events. He and his wife planned a trip to Alaska, Canada, and the West Coast. The Coolidges planned to return to New England. Grace Coolidge's father, Andrew Goodhue, died that spring, and the Coolidges attended his funeral in Burlington, Vermont, in late April. After stopping in New York and Massachusetts, they settled in at John Coolidge's house in Plymouth Notch on July 8.

On August 2, 1923, the vice president gathered hay on a neighbor's farm. He ate dinner and went to bed early that evening. Meanwhile, at about 7:30 P.M. Pacific time, President Harding, who had been suffering for a few days from what doctors thought might be food poisoning, had a heart attack and died.

Coolidge luck.

Coolidge triumphed over the scandals of the Harding presidency and was known for his honesty, hard work, directness, and good humor.

CHAPTER FOUR

MR. PRESIDENT

By my studies and my course of life I meant to be ready to take advantage of opportunities. I was ready, from the time the [Massachusetts] Justices named me the Clerk of Courts [in 1903] until my party nominated me for President.

—Calvin Coolidge, on his decision to run for mayor of Northampton, 1929

Just after midnight on August 3, 1923, a car with three men inside drove up to the Coolidge house in Plymouth Notch. John Coolidge woke up and answered the door. Calvin Coolidge later wrote:

> *I was awakened by my father coming up the stairs calling my name. I noticed that his voice trembled. . . . He had been the first to address me as President of the United States. . . . [T]he*

This painting depicts John Coolidge swearing in his son as president of the United States. Calvin Coolidge is the only president to have been sworn in by his father and in his own home.

———————— ✧ ————————

[presidential] oath was administered by my father. . . . The oath was taken [at 2:47 A.M.] in . . . the sitting room by the light of the kerosene lamp. . . . Besides my father and myself, there were present my wife, Senator Dale, who happened to be stopping a few miles away, my stenographer, and my chauffeur. . . . When I started for Washington that morning I turned aside from the main road to make a short . . . visit to the grave of my mother.

That morning Calvin Coolidge's son John was at Fort Devens, Massachusetts, where he was taking military training as a civilian (nonmilitary citizen). John was surprised when he found out at breakfast that his father was president, but he noted that nothing changed. Calvin Jr. was working on a Connecticut tobacco farm. Another worker remarked, "If my father was President I would not work in a tobacco field." Calvin Jr. replied, "If my father were your father, you would."

Coolidge went to Harding's funeral and stayed at the Willard hotel until August 21, to give Mrs. Harding time to leave for home in Ohio. He took an oath of office a second time (at the suggestion of Attorney General Daugherty), asked former president William Taft for advice, and got down to business.

──────────────── ✧ ────────────────

President Harding's body leaves the White House during his funeral procession in 1923.

"I THOUGHT I COULD SWING IT"

Calvin Coolidge had rarely left New England and never traveled to a foreign country except Canada. He had no experience with running a large business and had done little as vice president. Many people thought that he would be president only until the 1924 election, when the Republican Party would find a candidate to replace him on the ballot.

But Coolidge had been governor of Massachusetts. He had read a great deal and worked hard. When he suddenly became president, he recalled, "I thought I could swing it."

These were the cabinet members Harding had in office when Coolidge became president:

Attorney General: Harry Daugherty
Postmaster General: Harry New
Secretary of Agriculture: Henry Wallace
Secretary of Commerce: Herbert Hoover
Secretary of the Interior: Hubert Work
Secretary of Labor: James Davis
Secretary of the Navy: Edwin Denby
Secretary of State: Charles Evans Hughes
Secretary of the Treasury: Andrew Mellon
Secretary of War: John Weeks

Coolidge kept these advisers for the time being but set a different tone in the White House. There'd be no more drinking liquor or telling crude jokes. Cigars, however, would be allowed. Coolidge enjoyed smoking them. Coolidge kept White House expenses down, and he monitored what was prepared in the kitchen.

A 1926 advertisement in American Motorist. In the 1920s, cars were increasingly popular.

———————— ✧

Coolidge's careful ways contrasted with the lifestyles of many people in the 1920s. Americans bought expensive cars and radios and went to beauty parlors and the movies. The advertising industry urged everyone to buy, buy, buy. Businesses were doing well. Many Americans enjoyed a high standard of living (although high prices and low pay in certain industries made it difficult for some workers to earn enough money to support their families).

The first issue President Coolidge faced was a possible strike of about 150,000 Pennsylvania coal miners. The strike threatened to bring railroads and many industries to a halt. Coolidge asked his secretary to tell anyone who called with questions about the strike to speak with Pennsylvania governor Gifford Pinchot or with the U.S. Coal Commission. Governor Pinchot pressured Coolidge to meet with him several times to talk about the strike, but Coolidge did not want to get directly involved. Finally, Pinchot threatened to act on his own. Coolidge invited him to lunch on August 24 with Coal Commission chairman John Hays Hammond.

It's not clear what happened at that lunch. The governor thought he was free to settle matters his own way. He was angry when the White House reported that he was working for the U.S. government. The miners went on strike on September 1, but Governor Pinchot managed to get an agreement between the workers and their bosses. The mines reopened about two weeks later, and the president praised Pinchot for his efforts.

The coal miners' strike shows how Coolidge felt about the presidency. "[When performing] the duties of the office there is one rule . . . more important than all others," he wrote, "It [is that you should] never [do] anything that some one else can do for you."

On the international front, Europe was facing an economic downturn. World War I had hurt the economy in that part of the world. Political unrest appeared to be spreading from China to Nicaragua. The United States, however, did not seem very interested in international affairs. The government did not want to get involved in conflicts unless it would help U.S. business to do so. One of Coolidge's first foreign policy actions as president was to sign an agreement with Mexico establishing the General Claims Commission. The commission's task was to settle claims against one government for damage to property by citizens of the other government (in this case, claims arising from acts in Mexico between 1910 and 1920).

In December Coolidge set up a commission to study ways in which Germany might pay the United States the war reparations (payment for damages) it owed. Germany owed the payments because the country had done damage to U.S. citizens and property in World War I. One of the men on the commission was Brigadier General Charles Dawes. Dawes was a Chicago banker who was the budget director in the Harding administration.

COOLIDGE AND CONGRESS
Coolidge became president at a time when there was tension between the executive branch (federal agencies that carry out government policies) and Congress. In the fall of 1923, the Senate began looking into activities at the Veterans Bureau. It also began investigating the government's involvement in leasing oil-rich land to businesspeople. The investigations continued for months.

By January 1924, the Senate had uncovered the dishonest activities known as the Teapot Dome scandal. Senators called for the resignations of Secretary of the Navy Denby and Attorney General Daugherty. In the middle of the hearings, on February 3, former president Woodrow Wilson died. The nation paused to mourn his passing.

Congress ordered that the land leases to businesspeople be canceled and tried to force Coolidge to fire Secretary Denby. As the head of the executive branch, the president thought that he should decide whom to fire. But he accepted Denby's resignation and appointed Curtis Wilbur to fill Denby's position as secretary of the navy. Coolidge demanded that Daugherty resign as attorney general and gave the post to Harlan Fiske Stone. Stone was the dean of Columbia Law School and a graduate of Amherst.

Attorney General Stone replaced the director of the Justice Department's Bureau of Investigation with John Edgar Hoover.

J. Edgar Hoover

———— ❖ ————

Under J. Edgar Hoover, the bureau—later known as the FBI—became a strong force in fighting crime. Crime was on the rise in the United States because people were trying to buy illegal—or bootleg—liquor. In the spring of 1924, Coolidge signed agreements with other countries that would make it harder to bring illegal liquor into the United States.

The Teapot Dome hearings ended in May. In general, the American public did not blame Coolidge for corrupt activities that had taken place when Harding was president. They thought Coolidge was a serious and honest man—though still a bit of an odd stick.

Soon after the Teapot Dome hearings ended, President Coolidge vetoed (refused to approve) a bill Congress had passed to increase the amount of money the government paid to war veterans. He argued that the bill was too costly. Furthermore, he reasoned, fighting for one's country without pay was a sacrifice that citizens ought to make. Congress voted again—this time with enough votes in favor of the bill to make it a law despite Coolidge's veto. In June Coolidge signed into law a tax reduction bill and a bill that gave full citizenship to Native Americans. He posed for a photograph with four Osage Indians in front of the White House. The new law had little economic effect on Native Americans.

Coolidge (center) poses with Osage Indians in front of the White House in 1924. Though known for his silence, Coolidge was very accessible to the media, always willing to pose for photographs and holding an average of eight press conferences each month.

Coolidge also signed the Immigration Act of 1924. This act set quotas, or limits, on the number of people from various countries who could immigrate to the United States. The law reduced immigration in general and made it particularly difficult for people to immigrate from Asia and from southern and eastern Europe. The law also set up a visa system, which meant that people who wanted to immigrate to the United States would be screened before they entered the country.

Coolidge became more popular. People no longer saw him as a temporary president. As early as December 1923, Coolidge had admitted that he was interested in running for the presidency. Although Silent Cal was known as a man of few words, he was the first president to make wide use of the media. He held press conferences twice a week, let people take his picture, and made the first radio broadcast to the American people from the White House. During the first half of 1924, he made speeches and worked to get his party's support.

SILENT CAL IN THE MEDIA

Calvin Coolidge was known as a man of few words, and it's true that he was not long-winded. But Silent Cal, as he was sometimes called, did understand the power of publicity. He spoke nationally over the radio about once a month. He met with reporters more often than any president before him— about twice a week on average. President Coolidge sometimes joked with reporters about his quiet nature. During one press conference, a reporter asked the president if he planned to give a speech at a country fair Coolidge was scheduled to attend. "No," the president replied, "I'm going as an exhibit."

The president did dress up like an exhibit at times. He allowed the press to photograph him looking like a farmer and a cowboy (below left, with his wife, Grace), and he posed with his pet raccoon (below right, with Grace) and other animals. When asked whether this was presidential, he responded, "Well, it's good for people to laugh."

On June 12, the Republicans nominated Coolidge for president and Charles Dawes for vice president. One party member noted that Coolidge "never wasted any time, never wasted any words, and never wasted any public money." Their convention in Cleveland, Ohio, was the first national party convention broadcast over the radio.

A TRAGIC LOSS

Calvin Coolidge had the most important political job in the nation on Independence Day 1924. And chances were good that he would be elected for a full four-year term in November. At their convention in New York City, Democrats were having a hard time finding a candidate they thought could beat Coolidge. But for Coolidge, this was not a day to celebrate. His son Calvin Jr. was seriously ill and in the hospital.

Sixteen-year-old Calvin had been playing tennis on the White House lawn a few days

———————— ✦

Calvin Coolidge Jr., shortly before his death in 1924

earlier. He had on shoes but no socks and found a blister on his toe afterward. By the time the boy told his parents, the toe had become infected. The infection led to blood poisoning. There was little doctors could do for him. On July 7, he died.

Coolidge was devastated by the loss of his son. He later wrote, "If I had not been President he would not have raised a blister on his toe . . . playing lawn tennis on the South grounds. In his suffering he was asking me to make him well. I could not. When he went the power and the glory of the Presidency went with him. The ways of Providence are often beyond our understanding. . . . I do not know why [I had to pay such a high price] for [living in] the White House."

———————————— ✧ ————————————

The Coolidge family (from left to right), John, Grace, Calvin, and John Sr., poses for a photograph a few days after Calvin Jr.'s funeral. President Coolidge wears a black armband to show he is in mourning.

The Coolidges attended funeral services for their son in Northampton on July 10. They buried him in Plymouth Notch near his grandmother. While the president was away, the Republican Party organization kept the campaign going. Keep Cool with Coolidge! signs were everywhere. A song told voters to "Keep cool and keep Coolidge for the good old U.S.A."

Coolidge did give a few speeches and appeared in a campaign film, but his heart wasn't in the race. Vice-presidential candidate Dawes traveled fifteen thousand miles on a special train to visit small towns and big cities and to make speeches in person and on the radio. "Where do you stand?" he asked enthusiastic crowds. "With President Coolidge on the Constitution with the flag, or on the sinking sands of Socialism?" (Socialism is a political philosophy differing from the capitalistic system in the United States. Socialism is based on the idea of social control of goods and production, while capitalism is based on individual ownership of these things.)

The Socialist Labor Party, American Party, Prohibition Party, Workers Party, and Farmer Labor Party all had candidates for the presidency. But the only candidate that was a serious challenger to the Republicans and Democrats was Robert La Follette, a senator from Wisconsin. A group called the Committee for Progressive Political Action had nominated La Follette. Several political organizations and labor unions supported him.

Two days after Calvin Jr.'s death, the Democrats finally nominated West Virginia lawyer John Davis for president and Nebraska governor Charles W. Bryan for vice president. The Democrats and Republicans spent more time attacking La Follette than they did one another.

A 1924 campaign card for the Davis-Bryan ticket recalls the scandal of the Teapot Dome.

In August the former Allied countries (mainly Great Britain, France, Italy, and the United States), which had fought against Germany during World War I, signed an important agreement with Germany regarding Germany's war reparations. The agreement was called the Dawes Plan, after Charles Dawes, who was a member of the Reparations Commission. Dawes's work on the Reparations Commission made him an even more appealing candidate for vice president.

On November 4, 1924, Coolidge was elected president of the United States. He received more than 15 million votes. (Davis received 8 million votes, and La Follette received just 5 million.) Only about half of those who could vote had gone to the polls that fall. People seemed to be more interested in the antics of stuntman Alvin "Shipwreck" Kelly. Kelly made news that year when he sat on top of a flagpole for thirteen hours straight. Kelly later set the flagpole-sitting record by staying atop an Atlantic City, New Jersey, flagpole for forty-nine days! He started a fad that lasted throughout Coolidge's presidency.

After his election, Coolidge, who was still heartbroken over the sudden death of his son, finished the rest of Harding's term. When Congress met in December, he sent an annual message, and he continued to carry out his duties as president. With Coolidge's support, Alabama senator Oscar Underwood proposed a bill to let a private company operate a government-owned dam and a nitrate manufacturing plant in Muscle Shoals, Alabama. Automaker Henry Ford and inventor Thomas Edison were interested in using the dam there to create hydroelectric power for making fertilizer.

Nebraska senator George Norris had other ideas for Muscle Shoals. He wanted to use the dam's hydroelectric capacity to bring electricity to rural areas of the Tennessee Valley. Controversy over the dam continued into the 1930s.

Mr. and Mrs. Coolidge (left) pose with Vice President Dawes (right) and his wife on the day of their inauguration in 1925.

CHAPTER FIVE

FOUR MORE YEARS

*It is a great advantage to a President, and a
major source of safety to the country, for him
to know that he is not a great man. When a
man begins to feel that he is the only one who
can lead in this republic, he is guilty of treason
to the spirit of our institutions.*
—Calvin Coolidge, on the presidency, 1929

As 1925 began, Calvin Coolidge got ready to work with a
new group of advisers. Secretary of State Hughes left his
position and was replaced by Frank Kellogg. John Sargent
became attorney general when Harlan Stone was appointed
to the Supreme Court, and the Senate refused to confirm
Charles Warren (Coolidge's first choice). William Jardine
took over as secretary of agriculture. He became the perma-
nent replacement after Secretary Wallace died in office.

Coolidge took the oath of office on March 4. The day
was clear and mild in Washington, D.C., and Chief Justice

(and former president) William Taft administered the oath. The president's inauguration speech was the first one ever to be broadcast over the radio. In his speech, Coolidge said, "Here stands our country, an example of tranquility at home. We appear to be entering an era of [wealth] which is gradually reaching into every part of the nation."

He was right. The economy was doing well. National income was on the rise. Food prices were low (which was hard on farmers because they couldn't make much money from their crops but good for consumers because their groceries were more affordable). Coolidge aimed to leave well enough alone.

WHITE HOUSE ROUTINES

The president settled into a routine in which "all days were busy and there was little difference among them." He got up at 6:30 A.M., took a walk, and then had breakfast with Grace. Describing this routine, he once wrote, "For me there was fruit and one-half cup of coffee, with home-made cereal made from boiling together two parts unground wheat with one part rye. To this was added a roll and a strip of bacon, which went mostly to our dogs."

After breakfast Coolidge dictated speeches for an hour, then met with official visitors. On Tuesdays and Fridays at 10:30, he met with his cabinet and, he noted, "I rarely failed to accept their recommendations." At 12:30 P.M. on most days, the president shook hands with admirers and sometimes posed for photographs on the White House lawn. "On one occasion," he recalled, "I shook hands with nineteen hundred in thirty-four minutes, which is probably my record."

President and First Lady Coolidge greet attendees of a reception for
World War I veterans held at the White House.

Lunch at 1 P.M., often with guests, was followed by at
least an hour's nap before an afternoon of paperwork in the
office. Before dinner at 7 P.M., Coolidge took another walk
"followed by exercises on some of the vibrating machines
kept in my room." After dinner, he did more office work
until 10 P.M., when Coolidge went to bed.

Grace Coolidge kept the social calendar and was an
excellent hostess. She was thoughtful, lively, and entertain-
ing. In addition to the dinners the Coolidges hosted or
attended, the president held White House breakfasts for
Congress members and others, where he served pancakes
and Vermont maple syrup.

In the 1920s, three young girls present Grace Coolidge with flowers and a kiss. Grace was one of the liveliest, most popular first ladies of her time.

—————————————— ◇ ——————————————

FROM FARMERS TO FOREIGN AFFAIRS

These pancake breakfasts gave Coolidge a chance to talk about current issues and events. One topic Coolidge discussed was how the United States could improve its relationship with countries to the south.

In 1925 the United States, which had control over Cuba at that time, gave Cuba title to the Isle of Pines (a large island off Cuba's southern coast). The U.S. Marines who had occupied Nicaragua and the Dominican Republic had left. The United States' relationship with Mexico, which hadn't been very good, was also improving.

While the Coolidges spent the summer in Massachusetts, Secretary of State Kellogg worked with Mexican officials to settle claims of Americans whose property had been taken in Mexico. He also set up a meeting with Britain, Japan, and other nations to help calm unrest in China. Chinese nationalist leader Sun Yat-sen had died in March 1925. The man who took his place, Chiang Kai-shek, was fighting against Communist groups and warlords. Kellogg drafted a treaty with the new Chinese government that made it harder for other nations and foreign companies to interfere with China.

Headline-grabbing news that summer came from Dayton, Tennessee, where Charles Darwin's theories of evolution were on trial. In a packed courtroom in the mid-July heat, William Jennings Bryan prosecuted schoolteacher John Scopes for breaking a Tennessee law against teaching evolution in public schools. Clarence Darrow, an expert lawyer,

————————————————— ✧ —————————————————

Lawyers Darrow (left) *and Bryan* (right) *confer during the sweltering heat at the Scopes trial in 1925.*

defended Scopes. Although the jury found Scopes guilty, he was given only a small fine. Darrow was widely considered to have won the case. Five days later, Bryan died.

Returning to the White House that fall, Coolidge worked on a program of tax cuts and government efficiency. He wanted to reduce public debt and improve the economy, and he also wanted to spend money to help defend the nation. William Mitchell, a colonel in the U.S. Army, claimed that the U.S. military had not developed enough air power. He accused top leaders in the army and navy of neglecting the country's national defense. Colonel Mitchell was brought before a military court, found guilty of insubordination, and was allowed to resign from the army. But Coolidge took Mitchell's claims seriously. He appointed a board to figure out a better plan for air defense and appointed Dwight Davis to replace John Weeks as secretary of war. Coolidge also asked Congress to provide more money for aviation.

In general, however, President Coolidge did not like to spend government money. He was against the McNary-Haugen Farm Relief Bill, which aimed to help farmers by having the U.S. government set prices for some farm products and by selling extra farm produce to other countries. Coolidge said that the bill would be too expensive.

In his annual address to Congress that December, Coolidge expressed support for Harding's position that the United States should join the International Court of Justice (also called the World Court). As 1926 began, the Senate considered proposals to keep farm prices steady and to have the United States become a member of the World Court. Senators argued over the pros and cons of the McNary-Haugen bill. Participation in the World Court was an even more controversial topic. At one point, it even caused a filibuster (the use of tactics, such as long speeches, to delay the passage of laws). Coolidge decided to let the senators fight it out. Each senator was supposed to represent the wishes of the people of his state. Coolidge reasoned that if most of the senators supported a bill, that meant that most Americans supported the bill too.

On January 27, the Senate approved membership in the World Court with five conditions. The most important one was that the justices of the World Court could not force the U.S. government to carry out their orders. Coolidge sent the Senate's proposal to the court's forty-eight members for their approval and waited for a response.

In February Coolidge signed a bill that would cut taxes. While he worked at the White House, his father became very ill. Ever since he became president, Coolidge had asked his

———————— ✦

President Coolidge poses with his father, John, shortly before John's death.

father to live at the White House, but John Coolidge refused to leave Plymouth Notch. Coolidge finally got a chance to visit his father in March. Unfortunately, he arrived too late. John Coolidge died on March 18, just two weeks before his eighty-first birthday. Writing about how difficult it was to take time from the White House to see his dying father, Coolidge noted, "It costs a great deal to be President."

Turning to foreign affairs that spring, Coolidge settled a land dispute between the countries of Chile and Peru. He signed an agreement regarding France's repayment of money it owed to the United States. And he worked to fix increasingly difficult problems with Mexico.

On the home front, Coolidge signed a bill creating the Army Air Corps. The bill was a response to findings from the board investigating U.S. air defenses. Congress adjourned on July 3 without deciding whether or not to go ahead with the McNary-Haugen Farm Relief Bill. Coolidge gave a speech in Philadelphia on July 5, in celebration of the 150th anniversary of the Declaration of Independence. Then he went to the Adirondack Mountains in New York, returning to Washington in September.

After President Coolidge came back to the White House, he and Secretary of State Kellogg focused on the civil war in Nicaragua. In November the United States formally recognized the government of Adolfo Díaz. He was the leader of the Conservative Party in Nicaragua. Several years earlier, the U.S. Marines trained his troops when the marines were in Nicaragua. Mexico gave its support to Díaz's opponent, Juan Sacasa, the former vice president of Nicaragua and a member of the Liberal Party. Sacasa established a rebel government, with arms and aid from Mexico.

In December the increasing chaos of the civil war threatened U.S. interests in Nicaragua. Coolidge sent in the marines. The president defended this decision—with which many people disagreed—in a speech to Congress in January 1927. But Congress still criticized Coolidge's use of the marines. Other countries criticized the U.S. invasion of Nicaragua as well.

Meanwhile, President Coolidge did very little to persuade other countries that the United States wanted to join the World Court. All of the court's forty-eight member nations agreed to four of Congress's five conditions for U.S. membership, but a few nations would not accept the United States' condition about the advisory role of the court. Coolidge insisted that there was nothing to negotiate, and he refused to meet with leaders on either side of the issue. The matter of U.S. membership in the World Court was dropped.

On February 10, 1927, Coolidge said he wanted to have an international meeting to talk about limiting the development of weapons. He asked Charles Evans Hughes to represent the United States at a conference in Geneva, Switzerland, with Britain, France, Italy, and Japan. Coolidge hoped that the nations would agree to produce fewer weapons. If they did, he could cut down on the amount of money the United States spent on defense. In February the president also vetoed the McNary-Haugen bill (which Congress had finally passed) and signed into law the Radio Act of 1927. The Radio Act created a federal commission to control the airwaves.

At about the same time, Columbia University professor James Shotwell came up with an idea for a pact, or an

French foreign minister
Aristide Briand
✧ ——————————

agreement, between France and the United States. The pact would outlaw war between the two countries. French foreign minister Aristide Briand liked Shotwell's idea. It was popular in the United States as well.

While Coolidge thought the United States should get involved in Nicaraguan politics, he preferred to be more patient with China. Secretary of State Kellogg suggested that the United States and Britain issue a statement asking the Chinese government to protect U.S. and British citizens there. By 1927 the Chinese Communists were centered in Shanghai, an area in which many British and about four thousand Americans lived. Britain sent soldiers to defend the area, but the United States did not. Several months later, a gang disguised as laborers pretended to be members of the Chinese Communist Party in Shanghai. Paid by Nationalist Party leader Chiang

Kai-shek, they killed hundreds of Communists. The Communists who weren't killed fled Shanghai for Hankow. Kellogg continued to use diplomacy rather than force with competing Chinese governments.

In the spring of 1927, the president of Mexico told Coolidge that he would be willing to negotiate for a peaceful settlement in Nicaragua. Eager to improve relations with Mexico and to remove U.S. forces from Nicaragua, Coolidge agreed. He asked Henry Stimson, who had been President Taft's secretary of war, to serve as a special envoy (messenger) to Nicaragua. In May Stimson reached an agreement between both sides in the Nicaragua conflict. President Díaz would stay in power until the elections in 1928, and the Nicaraguans would turn in their weapons to U.S. forces for about ten dollars per weapon—a great deal of money then. In the first ten days of the agreement, Nicaraguans turned in nearly sixty-five hundred weapons, along with five million rounds of ammunition.

This agreement did not satisfy Augusto Sandino, a labor leader who opposed President Díaz. He started a guerrilla war (a war in which small units carry out acts of sabotage and harassment) against the Nicaraguan government. He stole supplies from rich landowners and left notes that read: "The Honorable Calvin Coolidge, president of the United States of North America, will pay the bearer $_____."

SURPRISES

What really captured headlines that spring was not Nicaragua or China but the pilot Charles A. Lindbergh.

Charles Lindbergh poses in front of his plane, the Spirit of Saint Louis *in 1927. At just twenty-five years old, Lindbergh became an American hero.*

———————————— ◇ ————————————

On May 20, he took off from New York in an airplane called the *Spirit of Saint Louis* and flew nonstop for thirty-three and a half hours across the Atlantic to Le Bourget airport near Paris. After making the first solo flight from the United States to Europe, Lindbergh was an instant hero. Coolidge sent the government cruiser *Memphis* to bring Lindbergh and his plane back to cheering crowds in the United States. Lindbergh was the first person to receive the Distinguished Flying Cross medal.

At about the time of the Lindbergh flight, Secretary of State Kellogg formally accepted Briand's proposal to outlaw war with France. Briand then drafted a pact for both governments to review.

It was summer again and time for the president to escape the heat of the nation's capital. From June through August, the Coolidges vacationed in the Black Hills of South Dakota. The president enjoyed fishing, hiking, and just plain relaxing. He was once quoted as saying, "Four-fifths of all our troubles in this life would disappear if we would only sit down and keep still."

On July 1, Governor Fuller of Massachusetts surprised the nation when he announced that he was creating a committee to review the court cases of two Italian immigrants named Nicola Sacco and Bartolomeo Vanzetti.

——————————— ◇

Fishing was a favorite pastime of the thirtieth president.

GERTRUDE EDERLE

When Gertrude Ederle met Coolidge in 1927, he is said to have remarked, "I am amazed that a girl [as small as you] could swim the English Channel." Others were amazed too. Nineteen-year-old Ederle—who was actually rather stocky—was the first woman to swim the channel (below). Hundreds of men had tried the challenging swim, and only fourteen had made it. She beat the previous record by two hours.

Ederle had started out from Cape Gris-Nez, France, bound for Dover, Great Britain, twenty-one miles away. Her skin was covered with oils and lard to protect her from heat loss and stinging jellyfish. As rain, wind, and stormy seas sickened reporters and family in nearby tugboats, Ederle struggled on. She used an American-style overarm crawl that many said would be too tiring for long-distance swimming, but she was determined to succeed. Ederle had won medals for the United

Ederle wasn't the first to break a record crossing the English Channel. Many flight records were also set for crossing the channel. The first balloon flight across the channel (right) took place in January 1785.

States in the 1924 Olympic Games and had beaten many world records, but she had failed to make it across the channel on a previous try. This time, her father, a butcher from New York City, had promised her a car if she could make the swim.

Along the way, Ederle's sister sang to her and passed her chicken broth in baby bottles attached to a rope. More than fourteen hours and thirty-five miles later (due to the bad weather), Ederle made it to Kingsdown, on Great Britain's coast.

Ederle came home to the largest ticker tape parade New York City had ever given one of its own. An estimated two million cheered her, and she became as famous an athlete as baseball's Babe Ruth. Recognizing her amazing popularity, President Coolidge declared Ederle "America's best girl."

Vanzetti (second from left) *and Sacco* (second from right) *enter the courthouse, surrounded by guards and a large crowd of onlookers.*

On July 14, 1921, a jury had convicted Sacco and Vanzetti of killing two people in a robbery in South Braintree, Massachusetts. The court sentenced them to death. Many thought that the jury had falsely accused Sacco and Vanzetti. They thought the men were victims of ethnic and political bias (they were both anarchists, or people who believe in having no central government).

Americans were in for another surprise announcement, this time from their very popular president. On the morning of August 2, 1927, Calvin Coolidge held his usual press conference in a Rapid City, South Dakota, high school.

After the conference was finished, he asked the reporters to return at noon. They did.

Coolidge asked them to line up single file, and he gave each one a piece of paper with this message: "I do not choose to run for President in nineteen twenty-eight." The message might have left a reporter or two wondering whether Coolidge was enjoying another one of his practical jokes.

On his fifty-sixth birthday, President Coolidge enjoys birthday cake with his wife, Grace, son, John, and favorite canine, Rob Roy.

CHAPTER SIX

RETURNING TO THE PEOPLE

*I fully expected to become the kind of country
lawyer I saw all [around] me, spending my life
in the profession, with perhaps a final place on
the Bench. But it was [meant] to be otherwise.
Some Power that I little suspected in my
student days took me in charge and carried me
on from the . . . neighborhood at Plymouth
Notch to the . . . White House.*

—Calvin Coolidge, on his expectations of himself
as a young man, 1929

We will never know for sure why such a popular president
as Calvin Coolidge decided not to run for another term.
Some historians believe that Coolidge thought the U.S.
economy was declining and he didn't want to lead the
country in bad times. Others say that the reason was his
deep sadness after Calvin Jr. died. Coolidge later wrote that
he was concerned about his wife's health and his own.

Nineteen more months remained in Coolidge's presidency, and he had plenty left to do. In his quiet, focused, and calm style, Coolidge set about doing them—or leaving them undone. On August 3, Governor Fuller declared that the Massachusetts trial of Nicola Sacco and Bartolomeo Vanzetti was fair and that they could be put to death. However, he granted a stay, or waiting period, until August 22. People pressured Coolidge to stop the executions.

The conference to discuss weapons production had taken place in Geneva on June 20, but France and Italy sent no representatives. The three other countries—Britain, Japan, and the United States—could not reach an agreement. The conference ended on August 4 without success.

On August 17, a group of Native Americans adopted the president as an honorary member of their nation. Coolidge continued his vacation in South Dakota and did not take action in the Sacco-Vanzetti case. Despite international pressure to stop the execution, the two men were put to death on August 23. More than fifty thousand people formed a funeral march eight miles long.

FINISHING UP

The Coolidges returned to Washington in the fall of 1927. They stayed in the mansion at 15 Dupont Circle while the White House roof was being fixed.

Dwight Morrow, who had become the U.S. ambassador (official representative of a country) to Mexico in July, worked to improve the relationship between the United States and Mexico. Mexican laws made it hard for foreigners to own land in Mexico or tap into Mexico's oil fields. These laws did not please U.S. oil companies. Tensions between the

Catholic Church in Mexico and the Mexican government also worried Catholics in the United States. Ambassador Morrow went to Mexico City in October to negotiate peace. In November the Mexican supreme court struck down some parts of laws, and U.S. oil companies could operate more easily in Mexico. A month later, Morrow brought Charles Lindbergh to visit enthusiastic crowds in Mexico and establish nonstop flights from Mexico City to Washington, D.C. Lindbergh would later marry Morrow's daughter Anne.

Meanwhile, with matters on the mend in Mexico, President Coolidge gave his annual message to Congress on December 6. He urged Congress to reduce both taxes and the national debt. Coolidge also stressed his position that the states rather than the U.S. government should enforce Prohibition laws. By 1927 many Americans wondered whether Prohibition was doing more harm than good. Deaths were on the rise from industrial alcohol that was not fit to drink. Crime was also on the rise as gangs fought to control the entry of illegal alcohol into the United States.

On January 16, 1928, Coolidge gave another speech. This one was at the International Conference of American States in Havana, Cuba. Thousands of people cheered the president and his wife as they traveled in Havana. The usually tight-lipped Coolidge was seen to be smiling. Some members of the conference wanted to pass a resolution that criticized the United States for sending troops to Nicaragua, but the U.S. members of the conference stopped the resolution. Later, a State Department adviser concluded that the Monroe Doctrine (which said that the United States would protect Latin American countries from invasion) was meant to apply only when European countries were also involved in those

President Coolidge speaks at the 1928 conference in Havana, Cuba.

—————————————— ✧ ——————————————

countries. This new restriction on the Monroe Doctrine became known as the Good Neighbor Policy.

The U.S. Senate resumed hearings on the Teapot Dome scandal. The hearings would last for several months. At the same time, Congress passed another version of the McNary-Haugen bill to protect farmers and a bill to provide for government operations of the dam at Muscle Shoals, Alabama. Coolidge vetoed both bills. This was the second time he defied Congress on the McNary-Haugen proposals. He said that having the government set the price for which farm products were sold "is [a foolish mistake] from which this country has every right to be spared."

In June Secretary of Commerce Herbert Hoover easily won the nomination for president at the Republican convention. Kansas senator Charles Curtis became his running mate. Their campaign slogan was "a chicken in every pot and a car in every garage." The Democrats nominated New York governor Alfred Smith for president and Arkansas senator Joseph Robinson for vice president.

That summer, which Coolidge spent in Wisconsin, Roy West replaced Hubert Work as secretary of the interior. William Whiting replaced Hoover as secretary of commerce. The United States promised to stay on good terms with the Nationalists in China, who seemed for the moment to have gained control of that nation.

On August 27, Secretary of State Kellogg signed the Kellogg-Briand Peace Pact in Paris. Kellogg and Coolidge decided that other nations (besides France) could also sign the pact if they wanted to. Fifteen nations signed in Paris that day, and nearly fifty more would eventually sign.

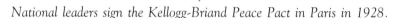

National leaders sign the Kellogg-Briand Peace Pact in Paris in 1928.

The Coolidges returned to Washington in September. The president gave speeches—including one expressing his love for Vermont—and continued with his duties. On November 6, Hoover won the presidential election in an easy victory.

DARKENING CLOUDS

Coolidge delivered his last annual message to Congress on December 4, 1928. He spoke with confidence about the strength of the U.S. economy. Coolidge had been successful in cutting taxes and reducing the national debt. He had even cut down on the number of towels in government washrooms in order to save money. But the good economy in the United States caused people to have too much faith in the stock market. People put a lot of money into stocks, believing that they would earn even more money. Some economists warned that the stock market would soon crash. Coolidge and his advisers, however, thought that people putting money into stocks could only make the economy better.

With just a few weeks left in his term, Coolidge got ready to move out of the White House. He had received many presents while president. As he later wrote, "Almost everything that can be eaten comes. We always know what to do with that." Coolidge had a reputation for liking animals and received many as pets. He kept dogs, raccoons, and other animals at the White House. His favorite companion was a collie named Rob Roy. Grace Coolidge had another collie named Prudence Prim. Coolidge sent many animal gifts to the National Zoo, including two lion cubs, a black bear, and a hippopotamus.

The Coolidges filled the White House with their favorite pets. In this photograph, Grace stands with Prudence Prim and an unidentified dog.

On March 4, 1929, Coolidge went to Hoover's inauguration and left Washington for Northampton, Massachusetts, that night. "We draw our Presidents from the people," he wrote. "It is a wholesome thing for them to return to the people. I came from them. I wish to be one of them again."

THE QUIET LIFE

After spending a decade in public service, Calvin Coolidge settled into a quieter life. He was elected to the board of directors (managers) of the New York Life Insurance Company and still had a law office in Northampton, but he did little work there. He joined the Northampton Literary Club and wrote an autobiography which first appeared as a series of articles in *Cosmopolitan* magazine.

Coolidge took up writing for newspapers and wrote a column called Thinking Things Over with Calvin Coolidge. Through his writing, Coolidge earned about two hundred thousand dollars a year—about three times his salary as president.

On October 24, 1929, the stock market crashed. The banks failed too. Millions of people lost their jobs and their

——————————————— ◇ ———————————————

A group of panicked investors flood the streets of New York City after the 1929 stock market crash.

life savings. Coolidge had little to say about the economy. He confided to a friend, "I feel I no longer fit in with these times."

But the Coolidges, who had always been careful with their money, moved to a new house in 1930. They left their rented home on Massasoit Street when curiosity seekers gave them little privacy. The Coolidges' new home was an estate with twelve rooms on nine acres of land. It was called the Beeches. Coolidge also became president again— this time of the American Antiquarian Society, a research library that focuses on U.S. history.

Coolidge did not leave politics entirely behind, and he kept his dry sense of humor. After making a campaign

———————————— ✧ ————————————

The Beeches (below) *in Massachusetts was a private postpresidency residence for the Coolidges.*

speech for Herbert Hoover in New York's Madison Square Garden in 1932, an enthusiastic woman stopped Coolidge. "Oh, Mr. Coolidge," she said, "I enjoyed your speech so much that I stood up during the whole speech." Coolidge replied, "So did I."

Hoover's Democratic rival, Franklin D. Roosevelt, defeated him for reelection. It was the end of a Republican era. In October 1927, the U.S. Supreme Court had ruled that the government leases of the Teapot Dome land to private companies were invalid. By 1932 several of the dishonest men who worked for President Harding were put in jail. Attorney General Daugherty went to court twice but was never convicted.

On January 1, 1933, Coolidge told a friend, "I am too old for my years. I suppose carrying responsibility takes its toll. I am afraid I am all burned out." Several days later, on January 5, Coolidge checked the mail at his law office, then came home because he wasn't feeling well. He worked on a jigsaw puzzle of George Washington, checked on the handyman stoking the coal furnace in the basement, and then went upstairs to shave. In the early afternoon, Grace Coolidge went upstairs and found her husband on the bathroom floor. He had suffered a sudden heart attack and died at the age of sixty. She had first seen him twenty-nine years earlier while he was shaving. Now this would be her last memory.

Funeral services were two days later, on a cold and rainy day, at Edwards Congregational Church in Northampton. Thousands of mourners came to pay their respects. Calvin Coolidge was buried near his family at Plymouth Notch.

*In 1933 mourners file past Coolidge's body as he lies in state in a
Northampton church before his burial in Plymouth Notch. This image is
the only known photograph of Coolidge's body.*

He had ordered matching granite stones for himself and his
son Calvin Jr. when the boy died, as well as a matching
piece of granite for his wife.

Grace Coolidge, who had taught at the Clarke School
for the Deaf before she married, continued to support the
institution. In 1935 she became president of the board. She
enjoyed baseball a great deal and was a loyal Red Sox fan
until her death at the age of seventy-eight on July 8, 1957.

GRACE ANNA GOODHUE COOLIDGE

"Alice in Wonderland or Babe in the Woods—however you wish to regard me—I'm here and nothing has happened to me." That's what Grace Anna Goodhue Coolidge wrote to friends in a letter dated August 21, 1923, shortly after moving into the White House. As First Lady, Grace Coolidge managed to handle whatever happened to her in a charming and outgoing manner. The Secret Service even nicknamed her Sunshine. After the sudden death of her son in 1924, Grace was able to carry on some of her public duties better than President Coolidge was able to.

Born in 1879 and the only child of Andrew and Lemira Goodhue, Grace grew up in Burlington, Vermont. She was friendly to everyone and had an elegant-but-unassuming style.

Her graciousness greatly helped her husband's political career.

In addition to her work as First Lady, Grace was a lifelong advocate for people

✧ ─────────────

Grace was so adored as First Lady that she received a gold medal from the National Institute of Social Sciences for her influence while in the White House. She was also recognized as one of the greatest living women of the United States in 1931.

Helen Keller reads Grace Coolidge's lips with her fingers.

──────────────── ✧

with disabilities. She invited Helen Keller, the famous deaf-blind author, speaker, and leader, to the White House. She also arranged for hearing-impaired children to attend Red Sox baseball games and raised money for the Clarke School, where she'd taught.

Another lifelong interest was baseball. Except during her years as First Lady, when she supported the Washington, D.C., Senators, Grace Coolidge was a Red Sox fan through and through. When she wasn't at the ballpark, she listened to the games on the radio. The First Lady's official portrait shows her in a long, elegant dress with her collie by her side. Missing from the painting is her baseball cap.

Reflecting on his mother, John Coolidge recalled that she "was game to try anything, and she loved something new, something different"—particularly after his father's death. But John usually preferred a quieter life.

THE COOLIDGE FAMILY

Like his father, John attended Amherst. A secret service agent accompanied him to his classes. After graduation, John married Florence Trumbull, the daughter of Connecticut governor John Trumbull. The wedding was held on a Monday in order to reduce the number of curious onlookers.

John Coolidge became an executive with the New York, New Haven, and Hartford Railroad, then later opened a business in Hartford, Connecticut. He also restarted and operated a cheese factory at Plymouth Notch, then sold it to the State of Vermont. The factory became part of a project to preserve and restore the Plymouth Notch area where Calvin Coolidge was born and spent much of his life.

John and Florence Coolidge raised two daughters, Cynthia and Lydia. Both daughters married and took the last names of their husbands, so John Coolidge was the last in the line of Coolidges to bear the family name. Lydia Coolidge Sayles raised a son, John, and daughter, Jennifer. Cynthia Coolidge Jeter, who died in 1989, raised a son, Christopher. When Christopher was a teenager, he contracted blood poisoning, the ailment that killed sixteen-year-old Calvin Coolidge Jr. in 1924. Because of advances in medicine, Christopher survived.

The Coolidge family worked to preserve Plymouth Notch. In 2000 John Coolidge watched as the old blacksmith shop

*John and Florence Coolidge (far right and right) posed with members of
the Coolidge Foundation and former First Lady Lady Bird Johnson (center,
in black) in 1995. John Coolidge presented Johnson with a signed
photograph of former president Coolidge's Plymouth Notch homestead.*

———————————— ✧ ————————————

was relocated to its original site across from his father's home.
A few days later, on May 31, 2000, he died at the age of
ninety-three. He was buried in Plymouth Notch, where he
often had often tended his father's grave—at least once pre-
tending to be simply the caretaker rather than the president's
son—especially around Calvin Coolidge's birthday on the
Fourth of July.

TIMELINE

1872   John Calvin Coolidge is born on July 4 in Plymouth Notch, Vermont, to John Calvin Coolidge and Victoria Josephine Moor Coolidge.

1875   Coolidge's sister, Abigail Gratia Coolidge, is born on April 15.

1885   Coolidge's mother dies.

1886   Coolidge enrolls in Black River Academy in Ludlow, Vermont.

1890   Abigail Coolidge dies.

1891   Coolidge's father marries Caroline Athelia Brown on September 9. Coolidge enters Amherst on September 17.

1895   Coolidge graduates cum laude from Amherst.

1898   Coolidge opens a law office in Northampton, Massachusetts, on February 1. Coolidge is elected to the city council on December 6.

1905   Coolidge marries Grace Anna Goodhue.

1906   John Coolidge, the Coolidges' first child, is born on September 7. Coolidge is elected to the Massachusetts House of Representatives on November 6.

1908   The Coolidges' second child, Calvin Coolidge Jr., is born on April 13.

1909   Coolidge is elected mayor of Northampton.

1911   Coolidge is elected state senator.

1914   Coolidge is elected president of the Massachusetts Senate.

1915   Coolidge is elected lieutenant governor.

1918   Coolidge is elected governor of Massachusetts.

1919 Coolidge intervenes in the Boston police strike.

1920 Prohibition goes into effect on January 16. Coolidge's stepmother dies on May 18. Coolidge is elected vice president of the United States, under President Warren Harding, on November 2.

1921 Coolidge is elected life trustee of Amherst on May 28. President Harding paves the way for the Teapot Dome scandal when he transfers control over naval oil lands to the secretary of the interior on May 31.

1922 The Veterans Bureau scandal surfaces on November 22.

1923 The Senate orders an investigation of the Veterans Bureau on February 12. President Harding dies on August 2. Vice President Coolidge takes the oath of office and becomes president of the United States on August 3.

1924 On February 8, Congress orders the cancellation of oil leases to private companies. Coolidge vetoes the veterans bonus bill on May 15. Coolidge signs the Immigration Act on May 26. On June 2, Coolidge signs a bill giving Native Americans full citizenship. Coolidge is nominated for president on the first ballot, with Charles Dawes as vice president, on June 12. Calvin Coolidge Jr. dies on July 7. Coolidge is elected president by a large majority on November 4.

1925 John Scopes is convicted for teaching the theory of evolution.

1926 John Coolidge, Calvin Coolidge's father, dies on March 18. On July 2, Coolidge signs a bill creating the Army Air Corps. Gertrude Ederle swims across the English Channel on August 6.

1927 Charles A. Lindbergh flies nonstop to Paris on May 20 to 21. Coolidge declines to run for president in 1928 on August 2. Coolidge is adopted by the Sioux Indians on August 17. Nicola Sacco and Bartolomeo Vanzetti are executed on August 23.

1928   The United States agrees to the Kellogg-Briand Peace Pact in Paris on August 27. Herbert Hoover is elected president on November 6.

1929   The Senate ratifies the Kellogg-Briand Peace Pact on January 15. Coolidge returns to Northampton after Hoover's inauguration on March 4. The stock market crashes on October 24.

1933   Coolidge dies of a heart attack in Northampton, Massachusetts, on January 5.

SOURCE NOTES

7 Donald R. McCoy, *Calvin Coolidge: The Quiet President* (New York: The Macmillan Company, 1967), 8.

9 Calvin Coolidge, *The Autobiography of Calvin Coolidge* (New York: Cosmopolitan Book Corporation, 1929), 33.

12 Hendrick V. Booraem, *The Provincial: Calvin Coolidge and His World, 1885–1895* (Lewisburg, PA: Bucknell University Press, 1994), 43.

13 Ibid.

14–15 Coolidge, 33.

16 Booraem, 78.

18 Coolidge, 47.

20 Ibid., 25.

20 Ibid., 52.

20 Booraem, 135.

23 Zachary Kent, *Calvin Coolidge* (Chicago: Children's Press, 1988), 31.

24 Coolidge, 65.

26 Ibid., 78.

26 Ibid., 90.

28 Cyndy Bittinger, "New Letters, New Insights Grace Coolidge, June, 2003," *Calvin Coolidge Memorial Foundation*, June 2003, http://www.calvin-coolidge.org/pages/history/grace/pages/letters.html (January 21, 2004).

28 Coolidge, 93.

30 Ibid., 100–101.

31 William Allen White, *A Pilgrim in Babylon: The Story of Calvin Coolidge* (New York: The MacMillan Company, 1938), 78.

32 Coolidge, 106.

32 Ibid., 107.

32 "Massachusetts Senate President Acceptance Speech, January 7,

1914," *Calvin Coolidge Memorial Foundation,* January 2001, http://www.calvin-coolidge.org/pages/history/speeches/sp010714.html (February 6, 2004).

34 Kent, 33.

35 Coolidge, 135.

36 Ibid., 121.

36–37 Kent, 35.

37 McCoy, 98.

38 White, 57.

43 Kent, 41.

43 Coolidge, 108.

44 Kent, 42.

47 Ibid., 49.

47 Ibid.

47 Coolidge, 159.

47 Ibid., 161.

47 Ibid., 162.

53 Ibid., 99.

53–54 Ibid., 173–177.

55 Kent, 52.

55 Ibid.

56 Robert H. Ferrell, *The Presidency of Calvin Coolidge* (Lawrence: University Press of Kansas, 1998), 39.

56 Ibid.

58 Coolidge, 196.

62 Parrish, 50.

62 Kent, 74.

63 Kent, 59.

64 Coolidge, 190.

65 Irwin Silber, *Songs America Voted By.* Harrisburg, PA: Stackpole Books, 1971), 242.

65 Ferrell, 59.

70 Coolidge, 173.

70 "Inaugural Address of Calvin Coolidge," *The Avalon Project at Yale Law School,* September 23, 2003, http://www.yale.edu/lawweb/avalon/presiden/inaug/coolidge.htm (January 21, 2004).

70 Coolidge, 200.
70 Ibid., 201.
70 Ibid., 204.
70 Ibid., 201.
71 Ibid., 202.
76 Ibid., 192.
79 Ferrell, 139.
81 Kent, 59.
82 Gerald Leinwand, *1927: High Tide of the 1920s* (New York: Four Walls Eight Windows, 2001), 271.
83 David A. Adler, *America's Champion Swimmer: Gertrude Ederle* (New York: Harcourt, Inc., 2000), N.P.
85 White, 361.
87 Coolidge, 79.
90 Kent, 76.

91 Michael E. Parrish, *Anxious Decades: America in Prosperity and Depression, 1920–1941* (New York: W. W. Norton & Company, 1992), 208.
92 Coolidge, 221.
93 Ibid., 242.
95 Ibid., 85.
96 Ibid.
96 Ibid.
96 Ibid., 86.
99 Bittinger, N.P.
100 Carl Sferrazza Anthony, *First Ladies: The Saga of the Presidents' Wives and Their Power, 1789–1961* (New York: William Morrow and Company, Inc., 1990), 473.

SELECTED BIBLIOGRAPHY

Booraem, Hendrick V. *The Provincial: Calvin Coolidge and His World, 1885–1895.* Lewisburg, PA: Bucknell University Press, 1994.

Coolidge, Calvin. *The Autobiography of Calvin Coolidge.* New York: Cosmopolitan Book Corporation, 1929.

Ferrell, Robert H. *The Presidency of Calvin Coolidge.* Lawrence: University Press of Kansas, 1998.

Haynes, John Earl, ed. *Calvin Coolidge and the Coolidge Era: Essays on the History of the 1920s.* Washington, DC: Library of Congress, 1998.

Kent, Zachary. *Calvin Coolidge.* Chicago: Children's Press, 1988.

Leinwand, Gerald. *1927: High Tide of the 1920s.* New York: Four Walls Eight Windows, 2001.

McCoy, Donald R. *Calvin Coolidge: The Quiet President.* New York: The Macmillan Company, 1967.

Moran, Philip, R., ed. *Calvin Coolidge: 1872–1933.* Dobbs Ferry, NY: Oceana Publications, Inc., 1970.

Parrish, Michael E. *Anxious Decades: America in Prosperity and Depression, 1920–1941.* New York: W. W. Norton & Company, 1992.

Silber, Irwin. *Songs America Voted By.* Harrisburg, PA: Stackpole Books, 1971.

White, William Allen. *A Puritan in Babylon: The Story of Calvin Coolidge.* New York: The MacMillan Company, 1938.

FURTHER READING AND WEBSITES

"Black River Academy Museum." *Black River Academy Museum and Historical Society.*
http://www.vmga.org/windsor/blackriver.html
Black River Academy Museum and Historical Society (located on 14 High Street in Ludlow, Vermont) includes photographs of Calvin Coolidge during his stay at the academy, as well as many other artifacts from the 1800s onward.

"Calvin Coolidge." *Calvin Coolidge Memorial Foundation.*
http://www.calvin-coolidge.org
The Calvin Coolidge Memorial Foundation maintains a large archive of materials related to President Coolidge, including his speeches and an extensive bibliography.

Feldman, Ruth Tenzer. *World War I.* Minneapolis: Lerner Publications Company, 2004.

Hakim, Joy. *War, Peace, and All That Jazz,* 3rd ed. New York: Oxford University Press, 2003.

Hanson, Erica. *The 1920s.* San Diego: Lucent Books, 1999.

"Historic Northampton." *Historic Northampton Museum & Education Center.*
http://historic-northampton.org
Historic Northampton Museum & Education Center provides a virtual or actual tour of the city in which the Coolidges spent most of their adult lives. The museum includes many Coolidge artifacts and interprets the life and history of the region.

Kendall, Martha E. *Failure Is Impossible!: The History of American Women's Rights.* Minneapolis: Lerner Publications Company, 2001.

Klapthor, Margaret Brown. *The First Ladies,* 10th ed. Washington, DC: White House Historical Association, 2001.

Landau, Elaine. *Warren G. Harding.* Minneapolis: Lerner Publications Company, 2005.

"Manuscript Reading Room." *Library of Congress.*
  http://www.loc.gov/rr/mss
  The manuscript division of the Library of Congress in Washington,
  D.C., has over 175,000 letters and other pieces of correspondence
  related to Calvin Coolidge. The reading room website offers details
  on how to conduct research on Calvin Coolidge and has an "ask-a-
  librarian" feature.

"President Calvin Coolidge State Historic Site." *The Plymouth Notch
Historic District.*
  http://www.dhca.state.vt.us/HistoricSites/html/CoolidgeTour.html
  The Plymouth Notch Historic District, birthplace and home of
  Calvin Coolidge, has been preserved for a virtual or actual tour.
  Several buildings have original archival collections from the late
  eighteenth to the early twentieth century.

INDEX

Amherst College, 19, 23, 24, 47, 100
aviation, 74, 76, 80, 89

Briand, Aristide, 78, 80
Bryan, Charles W., 65, 66
Bryan, William Jennings, 73, 74
business interests, 48, 49, 58, 59, 67

cars, 37, 38–39, 57
Chiang Kai-shek, 73, 78
China, 73, 78, 91
Clarke School for the Deaf, 27, 97, 99
coal miners' strike, 57, 58
Communism, 43, 73, 78
Coolidge, Abbie (sister), 8, 10, 14, 17
Coolidge, Calvin: advisers, 56, 69, 70,
  71, 91; appearance, 8, 16, 20, 24;
  childhood, 7–8, 10–15; death, 96–97;
  early political offices, 26, 29–30;
  earnings, 37, 47, 94; education, 11,
  12, 14–17, 19, 20–21, 23–25;
  governor, 36–37, 40–44, 45, 56;
  health, 8, 10, 19, 40; jobs, 12, 14, 16,
  26, 94; lawyer, 22, 23, 24–26, 32, 87;
  lieutenant governor, 35–37; mayor,
  30–31, 53; nicknames, 8, 23, 47;
  personality, 8, 13, 52, 88; pets, 62,
  86, 92, 93; philosophy, 32;
  postpresidency, 94–96; presidency,
  53–94; publicity, 61, 62, 70, 85;
  religion, 24; routine, 70–71; speeches,
  23–24, 26, 32, 43, 44, 92; state
  senator, 31–32; vice president, 46–47,
  56; wedding, 28; writing, 25, 45, 94
Coolidge, Calvin, Jr. (son), 30, 33, 46,
  55, 63–64, 97
Coolidge, Carrie Brown (stepmother),
  20, 44
Coolidge, Grace Goodhue (wife),
  27–28, 29, 33, 35, 37, 51; as First
  Lady, 64, 68, 70, 71, 72, 86, 93, 96,
  97; life of, 98–99

Coolidge, John (father), 8, 9, 13,
  14–15, 17–18, 19, 53, 54, 64, 75–76
Coolidge, John (son), 29, 33, 46,
  54–55, 64, 100–101
Coolidge, Sarah (grandmother), 14
Coolidge, Victoria (mother), 8, 10, 13, 40
Cox, Channing, 40, 45–46
Cramer, Charles, 50–51
Crane, W. Murray, 29, 31, 33, 34
crime, 41, 60, 89
Cuba, 72–73, 89
Curtis, Edwin, 40, 41
Cushing, Grafton, 33

Darrow, Clarence, 73–74
Daugherty, Harry, 48, 51, 55, 59, 96
Davis, Dwight, 74
Davis, John, 65, 66
Dawes, Charles, 59, 63, 65, 68
Dawes Plan, 66
Denby, Edwin, 59
Díaz, Adolfo, 76, 79
diseases and death, 8, 18, 37, 64

economy, U.S., 70, 74, 87, 92, 94–95
Ederle, Gertrude, 82–83
education, 12, 73
evolution, 24, 73

Fall, Albert, 48–49, 50
farms and farming, 11, 70, 74, 90
FBI, 59–60
Field, Henry P., 24, 25
flagpole sitting, 66
Ford, Henry, 38, 39, 67
France, 78, 91
Fuller, Alvan, 81, 88

Garman, Charles E., 24
Germany, 58–59, 65–66
Great Britain, 78–79

Hammond, John C., 24, 25
Hammond, John Hays, 58
Harding, Warren G., 45, 46, 47–50, 51, 55; advisers to, 48, 56, 59, 96
Harrison, Benjamin, 19–20
Hemenway, Ralph W., 35
Hoover, Herbert, 90–91, 92, 96
Hoover, John (J.) Edgar, 59–60

Immigration Act of 1924, 61
international relations, 58, 72–73, 76–79, 88–89, 91

Keller, Helen, 99
Kellogg, Frank, 72, 73, 76, 78, 79, 80–81, 91
Kellogg-Briand Peace Pact, 91
Kelly, Alvin "Shipwreck," 66

labor unions, 40
La Follette, Robert, 65, 66
Lindbergh, Charles A., 79–80, 89
Long, Richard H., 37, 43

maple sugaring, 11, 15
McCall, Samuel, 33–34, 35, 36
McNary-Haugen Farm Relief Bill, 74, 75, 76, 77, 90
media, 61, 62, 63, 70
Mexico, 58, 72, 76, 79, 88–89
Mitchell, William, 74
Monroe Doctrine, 89–90
Morrow, Dwight, 40, 88, 89
Muscle Shoals dam, 67, 90

Native Americans, 60, 61, 88
Nicaragua, 58, 76–77, 78, 79, 89
Norris, George, 67

oil, 48–49, 59, 88, 89
Olympic Games, 83

peacemaking, 78, 88, 91
Peck, Alva, 15, 16
Peters, Andrew J., 41, 42

Pinchot, Gifford, 57–58
police strike, Boston, 40–43
political parties, 20, 65
Pollard, Sarah, 15
Prohibition, 43, 60, 89

reparations, German, 58–59, 65–66
Republican National Conventions, 44–45, 63, 90–91
Robinson, Joseph, 91
Roosevelt, Franklin D., 45, 96

Sacco and Vanzetti, 81, 84, 88
Scopes, John, 73–74
Shotwell, James, 77–78
social issues, 29–30, 60–61, 84, 88
sports, 20, 24, 82–83, 97, 99
standard of living, 1920s, 57, 70
Stearns, Frank, 33, 36, 40, 44
Stimson, Henry, 79
stock market, 92; crash of, 94–95
Stone, Harlan Fiske, 59, 69
strikes, labor, 31, 40, 41, 42–43, 57

Taft, William, 55, 70, 79
Teapot Dome scandal, 48–50, 59, 60, 66, 90, 96
Turner, Alfred, 20

Underwood, Oscar, 67
U.S. Congress, 47, 59, 60, 74, 75, 77, 90
U.S. Constitution, 30
U.S. military, 37, 48, 59, 74, 76, 77, 79

veterans, 50, 60
voting, 30, 31, 45, 66

Walsh, David, 32–33
Wilson, Woodrow, 37, 42, 45, 59
women, roles of, 27, 30, 31, 45, 82
work and workers, 29, 30, 31, 38–39, 40–43, 57
World Court, 74, 75, 77
World War I, 35, 37, 45, 58–59

ABOUT THE AUTHOR

Ruth Tenzer Feldman has written several books on U.S. history and a biography of Thurgood Marshall. As a legislative attorney for the U.S. Department of Education, Feldman worked with members of Congress to pass presidential proposals. She lives in Portland, Oregon, with her husband, her Welsh corgi, and her trusty computer. You can find out more about her and contact her through www.ruthtenzerfeldman.com.

───────────── ◆ ─────────────

PHOTO ACKNOWLEDGMENTS

The images in this book are used with the permission of: The White House, pp. 1, 7, 9, 23, 35, 53, 69, 87; Calvin Coolidge Presidential Library & Museum, Forbes Library, Northampton, Massachusetts, pp. 2, 22, 27, 71; Vermont Division for Historic Preservation, President Calvin Coolidge State Historic Site, pp. 6, 17; © Hulton Archive/Stringer/Getty Images, p. 10; © Brown Brothers, pp. 11, 12, 41, 42, 46, 48, 50, 60, 68, 73, 75, 81, 86, 90, 91, 97, 98; Vermont Historical Society, pp. 16, 18; Historic Northampton, Northampton Massachusetts, pp. 28, 29, 63, 95; Wyoming State Archives, Department of State Parks and Cultural Resources, p. 49; © MPI/Stringer/Getty Images, p. 33; Library of Congress, pp. 36, 38 [LC-USZ62-26766], 39 [LC-USZ62-111278], 44 [LC-USZ62-128620], 52 [LC-USZ62-110629], 54 [LC-USZC4-2721], 55 [LC-USZ62-132074], 57, 61 [LC-USZ62-111409], 62 [right; LC-USZ62-100816], 64 [LC-USZ62-111381], 72 [LC-USZ62-131303], 78 [LC-DIG-ggbain-06797], 83 [LC-DIG-ppmsca-03478], 84 [LC-USZ62-124547], 93 [LC-USZ62-131573], 99 [LC-USZ62-111738]; © New York Times Co./Getty Images, p. 62 (left); © David J. & Janice L. Frent Collection/CORBIS, p. 66; Minneapolis Public Library, p. 80; © Bettmann/CORBIS, p. 82; National Archives (NWDNS-306-NT-157-062C), p. 94; Calvin Coolidge Memorial Foundation, p. 101.

Front cover: © CORBIS.